THE ELEMENTS OF SHAMANISM

Nevill Drury was born in England in 1947 but has lived most of his life in Australia. He is an internationally published author in the fields of mythology and alternative medicine. He has a long standing interest in the visionary aspects of the magical traditions, and he earned his Master's degree in anthropology for a thesis comparing traditional shamanism and modern Western magic.

D0187441

THE ELEMENTS OF

SHAMANISM

Nevill Drury

CW
11/24/99

ELEMENT BOOKS

© Nevill and Susan Drury Publishing Pty Ltd 1989

First published in April 1989 by
Element Books Limited
Longmead, Shaftesbury, Dorset

Third impression October 1989

Designed by Jenny Liddle
Cover illustration by Rachel Williams
Cover design by Max Fairbrother

Printed and bound in Great Britain by Billings,
Hylton Road, Worcester

British Library Cataloguing in Publication Data
Drury, Nevill, 1947–
The elements of shamanism.
1. Shamanism
I. Title
291.6′2

ISBN 1–85230–069–8

CONTENTS

'All that exists lives'

— *Chukchee shaman*

INTRODUCTION

I vividly recall my first brush with shamanic consciousness. In 1980 I was involved as a lecturer at the International Transpersonal Conference at Phillip Island, outside Melbourne, and it was the first time that many of the leading figures of the American human potential movement had visited Australia. Professor Michael Harner was a member of this group. A large bear-like man with dark eyes, a grey-black beard and an infectious chuckle, Harner had arrived at Melbourne's Tullamarine Airport carrying a shaman's drum, gourd rattles and a set of feathers and bones used by the Salish Indians for a mind-control game. Obviously he was coming in a capacity which was not purely academic . . .

My initial contact with him had, in fact, been more on an administrative level. Professor Harner had been the American reader for my Masters thesis in anthropology, submitted through Macquarie University. He had not only approved it but had recommended publication (it was subsequently released in 1982 in a modified form as *The Shaman and the Magician*) so I was really delighted to meet him in person. I gave my own lectures on the mythic imagery of the Tarot and then joined one of his workshops on shamanism.

This was the first time I had actually utilised shamanic drumming as an adjunct to visualisation. Harner explained to us how we could ride in the mind's eye on the drumbeat, how we could journey through a root in the World Tree – emerging into light

– and how we could contact our 'power animals' by doing this. It was truly wonderful to be able to do this in an urban setting. I felt quite inspired.

After the Conference, Harner held a one-day workshop in Melbourne and I felt I had to attend it at all costs. Here was an opportunity to explore shamanic visualisation more thoroughly. I had already made use of magical techniques of visualisation based on the Golden Dawn tradition and found it comparatively easy to hold images in my mind's eye. I was hopeful, therefore, that I could also gain some sort of experiential breakthrough into the 'shamanic reality'.

As I recall, we went all day without eating much food – I made do with just an apple and a piece of cheese – and for the most part it was simply a matter of journeying inwardly on the drumbeat. For me the initial contact, in a mythic sense, had come through the form of a hawk. It seemed to be a very tangible creature and I could readily sense its presence. It had powerful deep black and yellow eyes and a mix of black and brown feathers. I remember feeling quite reassured that this creature had volunteered to be my power animal!

Through the day, as I say, we continued with the drumbeat visualisation, breaking occasionally for shamanic dance, and we also played the Salish mind-control game as an entertainment. But the climax to the workshop, for me, came in the evening. Harner told us that he had been experimenting with journeys up into the sky, as well as down into the lower world. He asked us to imagine entering a smoke tunnel either by wafting upwards on smoke from a campfire or by entering a fireplace and soaring towards the sky up a chimney. As we entered the smoke tunnel, he explained, we would see it unfolding before us, taking us higher and higher into the sky.

At some time or other, Harner said, a water bird would present itself as an ally, to lift us still higher into the sky-world. Why this should be a water bird was not explained. He was also keen to see whether any of us would see any 'geometric structures' although he didn't wish to elaborate on this in case his comments had the effect of programming us into a specific visionary experience. As it turned out, several people in the group had visions of geometric, 'celestial' architecture.

The room was quite dark as Harner began to beat on his drum, and I found it easy to visualise the fireplace in our front room. Here is a transcript of my notes from this particular journey:

I enter the fireplace and quickly shoot up the chimney into a lightish grey whirling cloud tunnel. Soon I am aware of my guardian – a pelican with a pink beak.

Mounting the pelican's back I ride higher with it into the smoke tunnel. In the distance I see a golden mountain rising in the mist . . .

As we draw closer I see that, built on the top of the mountain, is a magnificent palace made of golden crystal, radiating lime-yellow light. I am told that this is the palace of the phoenix, and I then see that golden bird surmounting the edifice. It seems to be connected with my own power-hawk.

I feel awed and amazed by the beauty of this place, but the regal bird bids me welcome. Then the hawk comes forward and places a piece of golden crystal in my chest. I hold my breath deeply as I receive it, for it is a special gift.

The drum is still sounding but soon Michael asks us to return. However I am still high in the sky and find it very difficult to re-enter the smoke tunnel. When I finally do begin to return the heavens remain golden, and as I travel down into the tunnel I look up to see saint-like figures rimming the tunnel, farewelling me.

This journey was a very awesome one for me. After returning to an awareness of the workshop location and the people around me, I found it very difficult to articulate my thoughts. I seemed lost for words but anxious, nevertheless, to communicate some of the importance that the journey had for me. I felt I had been in a very sacred space.

My interest in shamanism has never waned since this particularly eventful day in my life. Prior to this time my enthusiasm for shamanism had been, in a sense, more theoretical. Intrigued by the visionary aspects of the Western magical tradition I had, for example, researched an earlier book comparing the experiences of Carlos Castaneda and those of modern esoteric practitioners (*Don Juan, Mescalito and Modern Magic*, 1978) and I also had a keen interest in the psychological uses of guided imagery. But it was the beautiful simplicity of shamanism that appealed to me. Also, the fact that so little was *imposed*. Here one could journey through to the light and encounter one's *own* mythic beings – spontaneous creatures of the spirit. It seemed quite different from the context of formal religion where one was *told* what to believe. In shamanism one could experience, firsthand.

Since 1980 I have been involved in informal shamanic meetings with interested groups of people, to share with them the shamanic drumming approach I first learnt from Michael Harner. I have also presented this method in more structured groups and workshops from time to time. However, one thing never ceases to amaze me – that within an hour or so of drumming, ordinary city folk are able to tap extraordinary mythic realities that they have never dreamed of. It is as if they are discovering a lost fairyland of cosmic imagery from within the depths of the psyche. During the 'sharings' which are a part of the workshops, all these marvellous revelations pour forth.

So I am very much committed to the idea of urban shamanism, of encouraging modern urban dwellers to explore these realities. After all, most Western people live in cities or towns and cannot easily visit the exotic and often isolated locations where native shamanism is found. Naturally, I was also delighted when Element Books commissioned me to write this book, for this is one way of reaching people who might be interested.

It goes without saying that I owe an enormous debt to the writings and research of such figures as Mircea Eliade, Michael Harner, Joan Halifax, Peter T. Furst, Carmen Blacker and Gordon Wasson, among many others who have pioneered the reviving interest in shamanism. Neverthelesss, it seems to me that there is room for an introductory overview aimed at a more general audience. That was the original intent behind *The Elements of Shamanism* and I sincerely hope it will help encourage still further interest in this fascinating subject.

At a time when we are all becoming increasingly aware of our environment, and the fragility of ecological balance, shamanism has a clear message – we should respect the sanctity of Nature. Shamanism also reminds us that our destinies on this earth are all intertwined, for we are all one in Spirit.

To this extent, shamanism offers a powerful and optimistic message and it is in our own mutual interests to heed its call.

Nevill Drury
Sydney, 1988

1 · ANIMISM AND BEYOND

Shamanism is a visionary tradition, an ancient practice of utilising altered states of consciousness to contact the gods and spirits of the natural world. When we think of the shaman the image of an enigmatic and mysterious medicine man or sorceress comes to mind – a figure who through entering a condition of trance is able to undertake a vision-quest of the soul, journey to the sacred places and report back to humankind on matters of cosmic intent. It may be that the shaman is a healer, able to conquer the spirits of disease, a sorcerer, skilled in harnessing spirits as allies for magical purposes, or a type of psychic detective able to recover lost possessions. At other times the shaman may seem to be somewhat priestlike – an intermediary between the gods of Creation and the more familiar realm of everyday domestic affairs. But whatever the specific role, the shaman, universally, is one who commands awe and respect, for the shaman can journey to other worlds and return with revelations from the gods.

To understand the essence of shamanism it is necessary first, however, to consider the earliest forms of religious expression, since we can then obtain a framework, or context, for the rise of shamanic beliefs and practices.

ANIMISM AND TOTEMISM

The earliest tangible manifestations of man's religious awareness have been found in prehistoric cave sites located in Europe and Central Asia. A Neanderthal grave discovered in Uzbekistan revealed that a circle of ibex horns had been placed reverently around the body of a dead child, and in a cave at Le Moustier in France, a dead youth was lain as if asleep with his head resting on his right arm, supported by a pillow of flint flakes. A selection of tools and bones of animals, left close to hand, suggested strongly that such implements could serve the youth in some future life.

It is possible that even at this early stage of human development Neanderthal man believed in a world in which spirit beings inhabited animals, rocks and trees, and conceived of some sort of afterlife in which his role as a hunter continued. Although such a conclusion is, of course, speculative, with the advent of the Upper Palaeolithic Era there is a clear indication that man had begun to think magically.

As noted scholar Abbé Henri Breuil has written, referring to the prehistoric cave and mural art of Western Europe:

> Animals are represented pierced with symbolical arrows (bison and ibexes at Niaux; horses at Lascaux), clay models are riddled with spear marks (at Montespan, a headless lion and bear, which seem to have received new skins at various times) – facts which evoke the idea of sympathetic magic. The numerous pregnant women and men closely pursuing their women suggest the idea of fertility magic. The deliberate alteration of the essential features of certain animals seems to indicate taboos. Human figures dressed up in animal or grotesque masks evoke the dancing and initiation ceremonies of living peoples or represent the sorcerers or gods of the Upper Palaeolithic.[1]

One of the most characteristic examples of magical cave art was discovered in the Franco-Cantabrian cave of Les Trois-Frères. Some 15,000 years old, the cave drawings depict a hunter-sorcerer armed with a bow and disguised as a bison, amidst a herd of wild beasts. Another example of a sorcerer wearing horned head-gear to deceive his prey was also found at the same site.

From early times, religion, art and magic seem to have been intertwined. The sorcerer was a master of wild animals – able to control their fate through his hunting magic, an adept at disguises, and a practitioner of animal sacrifice. He learned to mimic the animals and in turn based his dances on their movements, and he

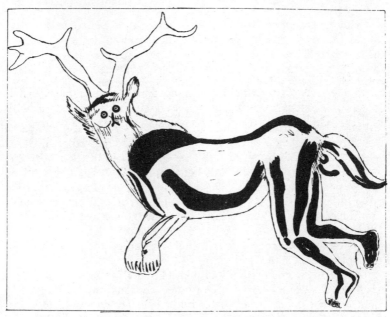

Cave painting of a sorcerer: Les Trois Frères, France

felt he had developed a psychic bond with them. In this way the Palaeolithic hunter-sorcerer was a precursor of the archetypal native shaman with his animal familiars, his clan totems and his belief that he could transform his consciousness into an animal form.

The pioneering English anthropologist Sir Edward Tylor (1832–1917) gave a name to the earliest phase of magical and religious thinking, calling it Animism, after the Greek word *anima*, meaning 'soul'. According to Tylor, the idea of a soul, or spirit, seemed already at this stage to be universal, and prehistoric man apparently believed that not only did *he* have a soul but animals and plants did also. In addition, stones, weapons, food and ornaments could also have souls and man's spirit could enter into the bodies of other men, animals or objects through an act of possession. Tylor believed that the origin of animism probably lay in the experience of dreams – which seemed to show that man could exist independently of his physical body. Today, certain native peoples still use a common word for 'shadows', 'spirits' and 'ghosts' reflecting the belief in man's dual existence. The Algonquin Indians, for example, call a man's soul his *otahchuk*, or 'shadow'; the Quiché say *natub* to denote a 'shadow' or 'soul', and the Zulu use the term *tunzi* for a shadow, spirit or ghost.

Tylor considered that once prehistoric man had come to conceive of two selves – the waking self and the phantom – it was a logical progression to believe that one's soul could undertake spirit journeys beyond the body or into an afterlife. Early evidence for such beliefs could be found in the remains of funeral rites where low-ranking servants had been sacrificed so that they could continue to serve deceased high-ranking officials in the afterworld, thus perpetuating the social order in the realm beyond death. Tylor also believed that primitive tribesfolk – 'savages' or 'rude races' as he so disparagingly called them – continued to reflect such animism in their everyday behaviour. It was animism – the belief in spirits – which would lead native peoples to converse with wild beasts, seeking their pardon prior to slaying them in the hunt, or to form a conviction that animals could have souls which, in earlier lives, had occupied the bodies of other human beings – possibly deceased friends or ancestors.

Tylor's overall concept is still highly regarded today, although it has not gone unchallenged.

The distinguished French sociologist Émile Durkheim (1858–1917) undertook a broad survey of cultural patterns and customs and believed that the earliest type of human society consisted of undifferentiated hordes. Later, the hordes became more independent and formed themselves into clans – a unit Durkheim believed to be more basic than the family. Durkheim was not impressed by Tylor's essentially psychological idea that magical and religious thinking originated from dreams. He believed that primitive man gradually came to conceive of the clan as the overriding social unit and that in due course it became 'sacred' simply because it represented a higher, more all-embracing reality than the individual. Indeed, he pointed out, when the clans acquired totem animals as symbols of differentiation, such totems were even more sacred than the actual animals themselves. Durkheim believed he could find evidence of this development process among the ethnographic data of the Australian Aborigines – the best-documented of the hunter-gatherer tribal people still surviving in modern times.

According to Durkheim, among Australian hunter-gatherers the totem animal or plant not only identified the clan but helped define patterns of kinship, since all clan members considered that they were related to each other. Durkheim also noted that Central Australian tribes like the Arunta had ritual instruments – *tjurunga* or *churinga* – which were sacred to the clan, and whose names were never revealed to strangers. Such was the potency of the clan as the basic social reality of the hunter-gatherer.

Today the distinction between Tylor's and Durkheim's way of thinking continues. Anthropologists tend to be divided into those whose frameworks of explanation are primarily cognitive or psychological, and those who emphasise the functional aspect of social roles. As one would expect, this leads in turn to different types of approach. An anthropologist evaluating shamanism from a psychological perspective will tend to be more interested in the altered states of consciousness accessed through trance, the visionary origins of the shaman's magical and religious beliefs and other factors such as epileptic seizures, schizophrenic behaviour patterns and the use of psychedelics, all of which are associated with shamanism. Functionalists on the other hand, are more inclined to ignore the experiential side of the shaman and his inner world, concentrating instead on the role the shaman plays in society by interpreting tribal customs and taboos, reinforcing the beliefs underpinning the social structure and providing guidelines for the tribe.

From my own viewpoint, there is no escaping the inner dimension, the awesome magical realm that in the shaman's cosmological system parallels the everyday world and fills it with meaning and significance. If we did not consider the role of familiar spirits, initiatory visions, the experience of magical dismemberment and rebirth, and the transformative projection of consciousness into other living forms like animals and birds, we would have a very one-sided understanding of shamanism. We could also hardly explain its mystique or account for the current rise of interest in shamanic states of consciousness within the modern human potential movement.

So with this in mind we should now ask: who exactly is the shaman, how does he or she become one, and what is 'the journey of the soul' which seems to be so central to the shamanic process?

THE SHAMANIC VOCATION

Shamanism is really applied animism, or animism in practice. Because Nature is alive with gods and spirits, and because all aspects of the cosmos are perceived as interconnected – the universe consisting of a veritable network of energies, forms and vibrations – the shaman is required as an intermediary between the different planes of being.

The idea of a universe alive with spirits is brought home in the journals of Danish explorer and anthropologist Knud Rasmussen (1879–1933), who undertook an epic three-year journey in the American Arctic regions. Rasmussen, whose own grandmother was part Eskimo, had a fine rapport with the polar Eskimos and was very interested when an Iglulik shaman told him:

> The greatest peril of life lies in the fact that human food consists entirely of souls. All the creatures that we have to kill and eat, all those that we have to strike down and destroy to make clothes for ourselves, have souls, souls that do not perish with the body and which must therefore be pacified lest they should revenge themselves on us for taking away their bodies.[2]

We can define a shaman as a person who is able to perceive this world of souls, spirits and gods, and who, in a state of ecstatic trance, is able to travel among them, gaining special knowledge of that supernatural realm. He or she is ever alert to the intrinsic perils of human existence, of the magical forces which lie waiting to trap the unwary, or which give rise to disease, famine or misfortune. But the shaman also takes the role of an active intermediary – a negotiator in both directions. As American anthropologist Joan Halifax points out: 'Only the shaman is able to behave as both a god and a human. The shaman then is an interspecies being, as well as a channel for the gods. He or she effects the interpenetration of diverse realms.'[3]

How, then, does one become a shaman?

Shamans are called to their vocation in different ways. For some it is a matter of ancestral lineage or hereditary bonds establishing the person in that position or a situation where a would-be shaman seeks initiation from one already established in this role. In other cases it seems almost as if the spirits have chosen the shaman, rather than the other way around. These are the 'greater shamans' – those who have been called spontaneously through dreams or mystical visions to embody supernatural power. Those who have simply inherited their role are regarded as 'lesser shamans' and hold a lower status in society, especially among the peoples of Siberia and Arctic North America.

To begin with, as children or young adults, shamans are often of nervous disposition and may seem strangely withdrawn from society. As anthropologist Ralph Linton notes:

> The shaman as a child usually shows marked introvert tendencies. When these inclinations become manifest they are encouraged by society. The budding shaman often wanders off and spends a long time by himself. He is rather anti-social in his attitudes and is frequently seized by mysterious illnesses of one sort or another.[4]

The Chukchee peoples of Siberia believe that a future shaman can be recognised by 'the look in the eyes which are not directed towards a listener during conversation but seemed fixed on something beyond. The eyes also have a strange quality of light, a peculiar brightness which allows them to see spirits and those things hidden from an ordinary person.[5]' Waldemar Bogoras, who studied the Chukchee at first hand, provides a context for this occurrence: 'The shamanistic call may come during some great misfortune, dangerous and protracted illness, sudden loss of family or property. Then the person, having no other services, turns to the spirits and claims their assistance.'[6]

Much has been made of the idea that Shamanism is born of crisis and disease, and it has also been compared with schizophrenia. Julian Silverman, who is a leading advocate of this view, feels that the main difference between schizophrenics and shamans is that shamans are 'institutionally supported' in their state of mental derangement while modern society, for the most part, regards schizophrenia as an aberration. He believes that there is a striking parallel between the two phenomena and quotes a psychiatric description of schizophrenic states to make his point:

> The experience which the patient undergoes is of the most awesome, universal character; he seems to be living in the midst of struggle between personified cosmic forces of good and evil, surrounded by animistically enlivened natural objects which are engaged in ominous performances that it is terribly necessary – and impossible – to understand.[7]

However, a clear distinction obviously needs to be made at this point. While shamans and schizophrenics share the ability to move in and out of different mental states, the shaman has gradually learned how to integrate the different realms of consciousness, thereby bringing matters firmly under control. As the noted scholar of comparative religion, Mircea Eliade, has indicated:

> the primitive magician, the medicine man, or the shaman is not only a sick man; he is, above all, a sick man who has been cured, who has succeeded in curing himself. Often when the shaman's or medicine man's vocation is revealed through an illness or epileptoid attack, the initiation of the candidate is equivalent to a cure.[8]

Eliade also elaborates on this point in his book *Birth and Rebirth*:

> The shamans and mystics of primitive societies are considered – and rightly – to be superior beings; their magico-religious powers also find expression in an extension of their mental capacities. The shaman is the man who *knows* and *remembers*, that is, who understands the mysteries of life and death.[9]

Clearly, there is more involved than just psychological aberration or disease. Because epilepsy and schizophrenia are regarded in primitive societies as manifestations of the spirit world it is not surprising that people suffering from these conditions could later become worthwhile shamans. But it is because they are open to the world of spirits and have learned to converse with them and manifest their presence that they are special – not simply because they are sick. It is only the person who has learned to master the inner worlds who can become accepted as a true shaman. Harnessing the power is everything – the crisis, or disease, thus becomes an initiation.

Shamans are expected very much to exhibit control of the supernatural powers which interfere with human life. This includes procuring game animals at times when the hunt appears to be failing, driving away evil spirits, obtaining good weather, and curing the sick. The Eskimo shaman, for example, has to journey in trance to the bottom of the sea to propitiate Sedna, the Goddess of the Sea. Sedna controls the sea mammals which provide food, fuel and skins for their clothing but she also unleashes most of the misfortunes that the Eskimo experiences. As William Lessa and Evon Vogt explain:

> These misfortunes are due to misdeeds and offences committed by men and they gather in dirt and impurity over the body of the goddess. It is necessary for the shaman to go through a dangerous ordeal to reach the sea goddess at the bottom of the sea. He must then stroke her hair and report the difficulties of his people. The goddess replies that breaches of taboos have caused their misfortunes. Whereupon the shaman returns for the mass confession from all the people who have committed misdeeds. Presumably when all sins are confessed, the sea goddess releases the game, returns lost souls, cures illnesses, and generally makes the world right with the Eskimos again.[10]

A distinguishing feature of shamanism, then, is the journey of the soul. It is because the shaman can project his consciousness to other realms that he is called a 'technician of the sacred' or a 'master of ecstasy'. It is this capacity to venture consciously among the spirits and return with sacred information for the benefit of society, that is all-important.

8

THE JOURNEY OF THE SOUL

In one sense, as we have seen, shamanism can be regarded as a controlled act of mental dissociation. It is as if the practitioner is able to travel in his soul-body to other realms of existence – harnessing familiar spirits, perhaps encountering spirits of death or disease, meeting with ancestor or creator gods and sometimes even participating in the mythic drama of the Creation itself.

This act of dissociation can come about in many ways. As we will see in subsequent chapters of this book, sometimes sacred psychedelic plants provide the impetus for the shamanic journey; at other times the spirit quest comes about following periods of fasting, sensory deprivation, meditative focusing, chanting, through the beating of drums, or through a particular response to a dream.

The *dehar* shaman among the Kalash Kafirs of Pakistan, for example, enters a trance state by standing immovably, relaxing his posture and then focusing his attention on a ceremonial altar to such an extent that every external element in his vision is excluded from his gaze. He then begins to shiver, jerks spasmodically, and enters an altered state of consciousness.

Singaporean shamanic candidates – mostly recent arrivals from China – become a *dang-ki* by displaying spontaneous signs of possession during temple ceremonies and then meditating on well-known *shen* divinities until the dissociational state is fully developed.

Among the Menangkabau, in Indonesia, it is considered that the life-force, or *sumangat*, leaves the body in dreams or during states of sickness, and that the task of the *dukun*, or shaman, is to counteract the hostile influence of evil spirits during the out-of-the-body state. Here the dukun summons friendly spirits through a smoke offering, lies down on the ground covered by a blanket, begins to tremble physically, and then project his consciousness into the mystical realm of the spirit world.

Meanwhile in the Mentawei Islands near Sumatra, shamans dance until they fall into a state of trance. They are then borne up into the sky in a boat carried by eagles where they meet sky spirits and ask them for remedies to treat disease.

Traditional Eskimo shamans, meanwhile, work themselves into a state of ecstasy by utilising the energy of a drumbeat and invoking helper spirits. Some Eskimos lace their arms and legs tightly to their bodies to hasten the release of the inner light-force on the 'spirit

9

flight', or *ilimarneq*. The classic case, however, is provided by Knud Rasmussen, the Danish explorer referred to above, who has provided us with the definitive account of an Eskimo spirit-journey.

The particular incident described in his *Report of the Fifth Thule Expedition 1921–1924* involved breaches of taboos which had invoked the wrath of the Sea Goddess. The shaman's role was to intercede on the community's behalf, travelling in his spirit body to the bottom of the sea.

At the beginning of the ceremony, members of the adult community gather around the shaman and observe him while he sits in meditative silence. Soon, feeling he is surrounded by helper spirits, he declares that 'the way is open' for him to undertake his journey. Various members of the household now sing in chorus while the shaman undertakes his difficult task: carefully avoiding three large, rolling stones on the sea floor and slipping nimbly past the Goddess's snarling watchdog. Rasmussen provides us with some idea of the perceptual process experienced by the shaman in his spirit projection when he writes that 'He almost glides as if falling through a tube so fitted to his body that he can check his progress by pressing against the sides, and need not actually fall down with a rush. This tube is kept open for him by all the souls of his namesakes, until he returns on his way back to earth.'[11]

The shaman now meets the Sea Goddess who, he can see, is nearly suffocating from the impurities of the misdeeds enacted by mankind. As the shaman strokes her hair to placate her, the Sea Goddess communicates with him in spirit-language, telling him that on this occasion there have been secret miscarriages among the women, and boiled meat has also been eaten in breach of taboo. When the shaman returns in due course to his communal comrades, it is this message he will relay and the offenders are sought out to explain their wrongdoing.

We can see from this account what is generally the case in Shamanism – that the spirit-journey is not undertaken purely as an indulgence. Always there is a clear task involved – to counteract sickness, to understand the nature of breached taboos, to recapture a lost or tormented soul, or to help restore harmony to the different planes of the cosmos, thereby easing the rift between the spirit world and members of the community.

This, essentially, is the role of the shaman – to journey to other worlds and to use revealed knowledge for a positive outcome. In this way the shaman is an intermediary between the gods and mankind.

2 · WHERE IS SHAMANISM FOUND?

Shamanism is an extraordinarily far-ranging practice, occurring in many different regions of the world. The classical source literature on shamanism focuses especially on Siberia, and the term 'shaman' itself has entered our language, via the Russian, from the Tungusic world *saman*. However, forms of shamanism also occur in North and South America, among the Australian Aborigines, in Indonesia, South-East Asia, China, Tibet and Japan.

Perhaps at this state we should also differentiate shamanism from mediumism – since both involve trance states. Essentially, shamanism is active and mediumism passive: shamanism involves a *going forth* of the spirit whereas mediumism involves a *coming in* of the divine force. In the latter category one thinks, perhaps. of the Pythian oracle of ancient Delphi who made divinely inspired pronouncements in trance at the Temple of Apollo, or of some modern forms of spiritualism, including 'channelling', where ancient discarnate sages are believed to communicate with the living through the body of the possessed trance medium. Also within this mediumistic category is the darker aspect of Voudou in Haiti, where the 'Divine Horsemen', or *loa* divinities, are said to descend upon the trance subjects during their ecstatic dance rituals and 'ride' them in a frenzy.

In mediumistic trance, subjects do not recall their visionary episodes, having acted as passive channels for the received revelations. In shamanism, on the other hand the ecstatic has full consciousness of the altered state, and takes full responsibility for what transpires during the visionary journey.

The following areas of the world are the main places where traditional shamanism is found. We will of course refer back to these source locations, and specific shamanic practices and beliefs, later in this book:

SIBERIA

This vast region – stretching from the Urals in the west to the Altai Mountains in the south and the Arctic Ocean in the north – encompasses tundra, fertile plains and rugged, mineral-rich mountain systems. It is also the home of many diverse and exotic peoples, including the Buryat and Goldi, the nomadic reindeer-herding Chukchee of the north-east, the Turkic-speaking Kirghiz, Yakuts, Uighurs and Altaians, and the Evenks and other neighbouring tribes in the Tungus-speaking region near the Yenisey and Lena rivers.

Here the shaman is both a healer and ecstatic who undertakes journeys to both the sky and underworld in search of fugitive souls that are responsible for illness. Shamans in this region also utilise divination and clairvoyance, and are sometimes capable of handling fire-coals without being burned.

Buryats distinguish between 'white' shamans who liaise with the gods, and 'black' shamans who summon spirits, while Yakuts contrast the gods 'above' – regarded as passive and comparatively powerless – with the gods 'below' who have closer ties with the earth. Yakuts believe they have obtained mastery of fire from Ulu-Toyan, who dwells in the west in the third heaven. This god also created birds, woodland animals and the forests.

The Altaian shaman sacrifices a horse, similarly addresses the Master of Fire, fumigates his ritual drum, invokes a multitude of spirits, and then calls to the Markut, the Birds of Heaven. After a complex ceremony of purification he then beats his drum violently, indicating that he is 'mounting' into the sky, accompanied by the spirit of the dead horse. After ascending through several heavens in his visionary consciousness, he converses with the creator god Yayutsi and also bows before the Moon and Sun in turn. Finally he

Yakut shamans drumming and dancing

comes to the celestial abode of Bai Ulgan, where he learns details of future weather patterns and the outcome of the harvest. The shaman then collapses in a state of ecstatic release.

Mircea Eliade notes that Bai Ulgan seems to be a god of the 'atmosphere' and it is not uncommon among Indo-European shamans to sacrifice horses to a god of the sky or storms.[1]

13

The Chukchee believe that spirits may be contacted in dreams and that shaman can utilise them to recover the lost souls of sick patients. The shamans is said to 'open' the patient's skull and replace the soul, which he has just captured in the form of a fly or bee.

Goldi shamans, on the other hand, specialise in funerary activities, guiding the deceased into the realms of the Underworld. The Goldi shaman calls on his helper-spirits for guidance as he accompanies the dead person, who is mounted on a sled together with food for the journey, toward the land of the departed. The Goldi subsequently locates relatives of the deceased in the Underworld so that the newly departed soul is safely accepted in the nether realms. Only then does the shaman return.

Evenk shamans also accompany the souls of the dead to the Underworld, where the deceased then lead a life substantially similar to the life they left behind – they continue to fish and hunt as before, although not visible to mortal eyes. Evenk shamans also use whirlpools to enter the cosmic river where they encounter the *khargi* spirits of the lower world. The *khargi* are able to assist the shaman to counteract the effects of evil spirits who are stealing the souls of the living or causing failures in the hunt.[2]

NORTH AMERICA

In North America shamanism is found, as we have already seen, in Alaskan Eskimo society, among the Tlingit of the north-west coast, among the Paviotso hunters, fishers and gatherers from western Nevada, among the Mescalero and Chiricahua Apache hunters of Texas, Arizona and New Mexico, the Lakota Sioux of Dakota, and also the Nez Perce, Ojibwa (also known as Chippewa), Zuni and Twana. Shamanic traditions still survive among the Pacific Coast Indians like the Pomo and Salish, the Chumash, who formerly occupied the region around Ojai, and native tribes like the Yurok, Wintu and Karok of north-western California. However, in native North American societies it has become difficult to distinguish between shamans and other technicians of sacred knowledge, like priests, medicine men and women, and sorcerers.

The ecstatic movement known as the Ghost Dance Religion, which flourished throughout the nineteenth century, brought a messianic emphasis to the native American tradition by focusing on the end of the world and the future regeneration of the planet by Indians, both dead and alive. The Ghost Dance Religion did exhibit mystical tendencies – practitioners entered a state of trance and dancers would often become healers – but it differed from traditional shamanism by making it potentially a 'collective' experience for its members.

Nevertheless, there are clear instances of pure shamanism. Paviotso shamans enter trance states and fly in the spirit-vision to retrieve lost souls and effect healing cures, and on occasion also hold shamanic ceremonies to control the weather – bringing rain when needed, halting clouds, or melting icy rivers. To this extent they are remarkably similar to their Siberian counterparts.

The Chumash medicine woman Chequeesh told researcher Will Noffke in 1985 that she had learned of her native heritage by utilising the 'dream herb', mugwort. At Point Conception she presented herself to the local healer, fasted for four days and nights, then went to a nearby mountain alone to use the herb to obtain her 'vision'. Her dream came, provided her spiritual name, and showed her the path of healing she should follow.[3]

The Yurok, Wintu and Karok Indians also pay special regard to their dreams for signs of omens, portents and psychic attack. In these native cultures, for example, the appearance of an owl in a dream could be a sign that an evil shaman was endeavouring to cause harm, and such an event – imagined or otherwise – would cause considerable stress and often ensuing sickness to those who had the experience. Sometimes a hostile 'force' is also conveyed by uma'a – a type of psychic arrow fired at night towards the victims – and a healing shaman is then required to suck these arrows out of the victim's body to effect a healing.

Apache Indians express a strong fear of the dead, especially dead relatives, and also of illnesses which result from contact with certain animals like bears and snakes. As with the northern Californian Indians, they also fear owls because they believe that ghosts appear in this form, and they refer to the illness resulting from persecution by ghosts either as 'ghost sickness', 'owl sickness' or 'darkness sickness'.

The Apache fearing attack of this kind may utilise the powers of a healer shaman who 'sings' over the patient to determine the nature of the bewitchment.[4]

The Paviotso Dick Mahwee, meanwhile, has described how he obtained his first shamanic visions during a dream in a cave near Dayton, when he was 50 years old. In a state of seemingly 'conscious sleep', Mahwee had a mystical encounter with a tall, thin Indian holding an eagle tail-feather, who taught him ways of curing sickness. Mahwee now utilises trance states in his shamanising:

I smoke before I go into the trance. While I am in the trance no one makes any noise. I go out to see what will happen to the patient. When I see a whirlwind I know that it caused the sickness. If I see the patient walking on grass and flowers it means that he will get well; he will soon be up and walking. When I see the patient among fresh flowers and he picks them it means that he will recover. If the flowers are withered or look as if the frost had killed them, I know that the patient will die. Sometimes in a trance I see the patient walking on the ground. If he leaves footprints I know that he will live, but if there are no tracks, I cannot cure him.

When I am coming back from the trance I sing. I sing louder and louder until I am completely conscious. Then the men lift me to my feet and I go on with the doctoring.[5]

MEXICO

Mexico is home to many shamanic cultures although, since this region of the Western Hemisphere is especially rich in hallucinogenic plants we tend to find an especially high incidence of psychedelic shamanism here. Examples include the Yaquis of northern Mexico who ritually smoke the yellow *Genista canariensis* flowers containing cytisine, and the Huichols who conduct their peyote pilgrimages in sacred country in the north-central Mexican desert. Also part of this psychedelic tradition are the Tarahumara Indians of Chihuahua who sometimes add *Datura inoxia* to the fermented maize drink *tesguino*.

A number of Mexican Indian tribes also consume sacred mushrooms as part of their vision quest and these include the Mazatecs, Chinantecs, Zapotecs, and Mixtecs, all of whom come from Oaxaca. The subject of shamanism and sacred plants is discussed in Chapter 5.

SOUTH AMERICA

This region is characterised by many exotic healing practices, not all of them shamanic. The distinction between a *curandero* and shaman is not always clear and there are also various spiritist traditions which are unrelated to shamanism. For example, the practices of French spiritualist Allan Kardec have been very influential in Brazil, as has Macumba – a magical religion similar to Haitian Voudou which combines native folk superstitions, African animism and aspects of Christianity.

As in Mexico, shamanism in South America tends to be psychedelic, making frequent use of tropical plants which contain hallucinogenic alkaloids. *Banisteriopsis* vine is widely utilised by South American shamans in the forests of the Upper Amazon, for the visions it produces are believed to represent encounters with supernatural forces. This is the case with the Jivaro of Ecuador, the Shipibo-Conibo, Campa, Sharanahua and Cashinahua of eastern Peru, and the Sione Indians of eastern Colombia.

The celebrated Eduardo Calderón, a Peruvian artist and shaman who was the subject of an anthropological documentary, *Eduardo the Healer*, uses the hallucinogenic San Pedro cactus, which has been in continuous use in Peruvian shamanism for an estimated three thousand years. Calderón is something of a special case, combining shamanic trance visions with prayers and invocations to Jesus Christ, the Virgin Mary and other important figures from the Christian tradition. See Chapter 5.

AUSTRALIA

Among Australian Aborigines the shaman or medicine-man is known as the *karadji*, or 'clever man'. Aboriginal culture extends back at least 40,000 years and it is thought that the Aborigines probably migrated to Australia from southern India, reaching Cape York via the Malay Peninsula and the East Indies. Today the principal regions where traditional Aboriginal religion is still found are Arnhem Land, in central North Australia and in the Central Australian desert – although there are scattered communities in other regions.

For the Australian Aborigines, illness, death and accidents are caused by magical or animistic actions and the shaman operates in a world where both imitative and contagious magic are practised.[6] Australian Aboriginal magicians also know how to 'sing' a person to death and 'point the bone' – type of projective magic where a kangaroo bone or carefully prepared stick is pointed at the intended victim.

The shamanic aspect of Australian Aboriginal culture becomes more obvious when we consider the initiation of medicine-men. Among the Arunta, or Aranda, the candidate goes to the mouth of a particular cave where he is 'noticed' by the spirits of the Dreamtime. They throw an invisible lance at him, which pierces his neck and tongue, and another which passes through his head from ear to ear. Dropping down 'dead' he is now carried by the spirits into the cave and his internal organs replaced with new ones, together with a supply of magical quartz crystals upon which his 'power' will later depend. When he rejoins his people as a person 'reborn', he has a new status as a healer-shaman, although he will not normally perform as a *karadji* for a year or so.

The power of the crystals stems from the fact that they are believed to embody the essence of Baiame, the All-Father or Great Sky-God of the Australian people. The Wiradjeri Aborigines of western New South Wales describe Baiame in reverent terms and one of their legends had a clearly shamanic perspective. For the Wiradjeri, Baiame is a very great old man, with a long beard, sitting in his camp with his legs under him. Two great quartz crystals extend from his shoulders to the sky above him. Baiame sometimes appears to the Aborigines in their dreams. He causes a sacred waterfall of liquid quartz to pour over their bodies, absorbing them totally. Then they grow wings replacing their arms. Later the dreamer learns to fly and Baiame sinks a piece of magical quartz into his forehead to enable him to see inside physical objects. Subsequently an inner flame and a heavenly cord are also incorporated into the body of the new shaman.

Crystals are also a feature of the Chepara tribe in Queensland. Medicine-men here are said to fly up to heaven after swallowing quartz crystals, and are also able to send rain through their contact with Targan, lord of the Rainbow. Wurunjeri medicine-men, meanwhile, maintain that their magical powers come from the sky-being Bunjil, to whom they were carried by spirits through a hole in the sky. The sky country is also the land of the dead.

As in Siberia and North America, Aboriginal shamans also learn of magical portents through dreams, and there are instances where initiates appear to use out-of-the-body states to perceive events at a distance.[7] It is likely that bullroarers are also used by shamans to produce an altered state of consciousness which can be utilised magically. The bull-roarer is swung around in the air producing a unique sound which is said to be the voice of Baiame, and those present stare into the fire in the middle of the sacred circle. Visions then begin to appear in the flames. 'Clever men' are said to be able to roll in the fire and scatter hot coals without being burned, and shamans also employ an invisible cord of flame which links them with Baiame and helps them to travel up into the sky. In these respects, Australian Aboriginal beliefs and practices have all the hallmarks of classic shamanism.

INDONESIA AND MALAYSIA

Shamans here exhibit many of the familiar characteristics found elsewhere in the world – including trance states, magical flight and contacts with spirits.

Menangkabau shamans seek their visions by travelling deep into the jungle or to the top of high mountains, while among the Iban, shamans undertake a fast, sleep near a grave or travel to a mountaintop until magical powers are obtained from a guardian spirit. The Iban also refer to the initiation of shamans through a metaphysical 're-structuring' process which has strong parallels with the Aboriginal account referred to above:

> they cut his head open, take out his brains, wash and restore them, to give him a clear mind to penetrate into the mysteries of evil spirits and the intricacies of disease; they insert gold dust into his eyes to give him keenness and strength of sight powerful enough to see the soul wherever it may have wandered; they plant barbed hooks on the tips of his fingers to enable him to seize the soul and hold it fast; and lastly they pierce his heart with an arrow to make him tender-hearted and full of sympathy with the sick and suffering.[8]

Dyaks also refer in their legends to somewhat shamanic journeys to the sky. The god Tupa-Jing noticed that the Dyaks were on the verge of exterminating themselves because they had no remedies for sickness and were cremating ill people as their only solution. He therefore saved a woman from the funeral pyre as she ascended in clouds of smoke, took her to heaven, and instructed her in the skills of medicine. Then she was able to return to earth and pass on the precious knowledge she had obtained.

Notions of spirits and sickness also parallel those found in other shamanic cultures.

The Sumatran Kubu believe that sickness arises when a person's soul is captured by a ghost. Shamans, known here as *malims*, are called in to effect an exorcism. During the seance the malims dance, fall into a trance, and the chief malim is then able to 'see' the patient's soul and retrieve it.

There are also instances, as in Siberia, where shamans journey to the nether regions. This is the case among the Dyaks, where the *manang*, or shaman-healer, falls into a trance state during a *belian*, or curing ceremony, and journeys to the underworld to retrieve a soul that has been captured by a spirit. Sometimes it is necessary for the *manang* to lure the evil demon back to the patient's house and kill it.

Meanwhile, among the Karo Bataks, when a person dies, a female shaman dances herself into a state of ecstasy and then explains to the soul that it has passed through the process of death. At a later ceremony she then sends the discarnate soul off to the land of the dead.[9]

EASTERN ASIA AND THE ORIENT

Here shamanism and animism pre-date the more familiar and mainstream religious philosophies like Buddhism and Confucianism.

In Tibet, Bon shamans speak of a sacred rope which in times past linked the priests with the celestial dwelling of the gods, and even today they are believed to use their drums to propel themselves through the air. As with other forms of shamanism, healers here similarly undertake the search for the patient's soul if this is perceived as a cause of sickness.

The Lolo of southern Yunnan also believe that in earlier times men moved more freely between heaven and earth. Among these people the shaman-priest also officiates in funerary rituals, 'opening the bridge to heaven' and helping the deceased find their way across various mountains and rivers to the Tree of Thought and other post-mortem regions beyond. Influenced by Chinese magic, the shamans of Yunnan also practise divination and undertake visionary journeys on horseback to retrieve lost souls.

In China, when Confucianiam was established as the State religion in the first century, ecstatics, shamans and diviners were banished, and some were killed. However, some shamanic vestiges remain in the Taoist tradition which is still served by monastaries and temples throughout the country. Ch'u State, in particular, has been a stronghold of Chinese shamanism.

The most obvious link between Taoism and shamanism is found in the meditative practices. Taoists use incense to carry their prayers to heaven, strike pieces of wood together in a monotonous rhythm rather like Siberian shamans with their drums, and believe that they can discover a spirit guide in the 'cave' of the heart. As the meditative state becomes experientially more real with increasing skills of visualisation and breath control, the Taoist then journeys with the spirit guide to distant mystic realms – perhaps communicating with the gods who live in the stars. In so doing, the Taoist meditator is behaving exactly like a shaman.[10]

According to Larry G. Peters, the Tamangs of Nepal also practise an authentic form of shamanism which, though drawing on elements of Hinduism and Buddhism, appears to pre-date them as a spiritual tradition. Peters' key informant, Bhirendra, was the son of a *bombo*, or shaman, and when he was 13 he experienced a spontaneous state of demonic possession which led to his initiatory calling. Under the guidance of his father, and also the spirit of his deceased grandfather,

Bhirendra learned to enter trance states voluntarily and in due course to activate the spiritual light between the eye – a condition leading to magical, out-of-the-body flight. Bhirendra described to Peters a vision in which he journeyed to the highest heaven to meet the supreme shaman deity, Ghesar Gyalpo:

> I walked into a beautiful garden with flowers of many different colours. There was also a pond and golden glimmery trees. Next to the pond was a very tall building which reached up into the sky. It had a golden staircase of nine steps leading to the top. I climbed the nine steps and saw Ghesar Gyalpo at the top, sitting on his white throne which was covered with soul flowers. He was dressed in white and his face was all white. He had long hair and a white crown. He gave me milk to drink and told me that I would attain much *shakti* to be used for the good of my people.[11]

Shamanism is also found in isolated regions of Japan, which is not surprising since it seems likely that Tungusic and Altaic-speaking tribes exerted a cultural influence on Japan, prior to the advent of Buddhism, in the third or fourth centuries. Shamanesses, or *miko* – more common than male shamans – are still found in small villages where they utilise trance, telepathy, mediumship and fortune-telling and communicate with guardian deities or spirits of the dead. In the larger cities, however, the role of the shamaness has been absorbed by Shinto ritual.

However, it is clear that shamanic episodes can still occur in modern times, as evidenced by the remarkable case of Deguchi Onisaburo which gave rise to the Omoto religious movement in Japan.

In 1898, Deguchi, who was by all accounts a frail youth, was beaten up by some gamblers and nearly died. A short while later he sank into a comatose sleep and on recovering consciousness declared that he had journeyed to a cave on Mount Takakura and after fasting there had travelled through regions of Heaven and Hell. On his journey he had been granted occult powers such as clairvoyance and clairaudience and had seen back as far as the creation of the world. His visionary experiences included a meeting with the King of the Underworld who in a moment was able to transform from a white-haired old man with a gentle face into a frightening demonic monarch with a bright red face, eyes like mirrors and a tongue of flame. Deguchi was subsequently 'killed, split in half with a sharp blade like a pear, dashed to pieces on rocks, frozen, burnt, engulfed in avalanches of snow [and] turned into a goddess' and yet, despite all these bizarre occurrences he then found himself at the centre of

21

the world, at the summit of the huge axial mountain Sumeru. Here he was granted a vision of the river leading towards paradise. Before him on a vast lotus stood a marvellous palace of gold, agate and jewels. All around him were blue mountains and the golden lapping waves of a lake, and golden doves flew above him in the air.[12]

Somewhat unfortunately, Deguchi's experiences led to messianic claims. During World War One he proclaimed that he was an incarnation of Maitreya – the future Buddha destined to descend from Tusita Heaven to save the human race – and he also advocated a form of spiritual healing which involved meditative union with the gods. In due course Deguchi's writings extended to over eighty volumes. His sect is still in existence, even though Deguchi died in 1948 at the age of 78.

3 • SHAMANIC

COSMOLOGIES

Obviously mythologies, cultural heroes and deities differ around the world and the relationship between the gods and mankind is perceived in different ways. Some peoples view their gods as tyrannical overlords, others as helpful parental overseers, while still others view their deities as supernatural beings whose power can be usurped with appropriate chants or invocations.

Despite these differences, when we eliminate cultural variables there seems to be a remarkable consensus in shamanic societies about how the universe is structured. As Mircea Eliade has indicated in his important work *Shamanism: Archaic Techniques of Ecstasy* – a scholarly reference volume which has influenced virtually all shamanic research since its first publication in Paris in 1951 – the shaman's universe consists basically of three levels. Man lives on the earth in a type of middle zone between an upper world and a lower world, the latter often associated with the sky and underworld respectively. The three zones are usually linked by a central vertical axis, which is sometimes referred to as the *Axis Mundi*, or Axis of the World, and which is characterised in different mythologies as the World Tree, the Tree of Life and so on. This Axis passes upwards and downwards through 'holes' in the cosmic vault which lead to the upper and lower worlds, and it is through these that the shaman is able to pass from one level of existence to another, and back again.

As Eliade notes, different cultures employ different metaphors and symbols to describe these zones. The Turko-Tatars view the sky as a tent, with the stars as 'holes' for light, while the Yakuts describe stars as 'windows of the world'. The Pole Star is often considered to be the centre of the celestial vault and is variously labelled as 'Sky Nail' by the Samoyed, the 'Golden Pillar' by the Mongols and Buryats and the 'Iron Pillar' by the Kirghiz.[1]

In those societies where the symbolism of a pillar or axis reaching to heaven is not utilised there are other variants like cosmic mountains, ziggurats, temples, palaces, bridges, stairs, ladders and rainbows or, as with the Evenks, a mighty river which joins the three levels of the cosmos. Always, the shaman has some means of ascending to the cosmic skies or journeying to the underworld.

LINKS BETWEEN HEAVEN AND EARTH

Cosmic mountains are found in Indian mythology – Mount Meru being considered the 'centre of the world' – and also feature in the legends of ancient Mesopotamia and other regions of the Middle East.

World Trees are quite common in Central and North Asian religion. The Yakuts of Siberia, for example, believe a tree with eight branches rises from the 'golden navel of the earth' and reaches up to heaven. The first man was born here, and was suckled by a woman who half-emerged from the trunk. The Goldi and Dolgan, meanwhile, believe that prior to being born, the souls of little children sit like birds on the branches of the World Tree and that shamans go there to find them.[2]

The World Tree is also a feature of Norse mythology: Yggdrasil was the sacred ash tree which overshadowed the entire universe, its roots, branches and trunk uniting heaven, earth and the nether regions. According to Norse cosmology, the roots of Yggdrasil lay in Hel, while the trunk ascended through Midgard, the earth. Rising through the mountain known as Asgard, the sacred tree branched high into the sky – its leaves being clouds in the sky, and its fruits the stars.

The Osmanli Turks talk of a Tree of Life which has a million leaves, each one containing a human fate. Every time a person dies, a leaf falls.[3] The Tree of Life is also a central theme in the Jewish mystical Kabbalah, a complex symbol describing the levels of existence between the transcendent Hidden God in *Ain Soph Aur* – the Limitless Light – and the ten lower *sephiroth* or spheres of being which reflect aspects of God's divine nature in the manifested world of creation. For the Kabbalist, as for the shaman, the essential mystical purpose is to know God, and although the animistic frameworks of shamanism are less ethereal and more pragmatic than the quest of the devotional Jewish mystic, it is worth noting that the Kabbalistic Tree of Life has also provided a practical focus for modern Western magic – which in one sense is a type of contemporary shamanism.

The World Tree also features in Dyak mythology, where it has seven branches and provides a 'road to the sky' for the spirits of the dead, and in like fashion Indonesian shamans climb the cosmic tree to retrieve the lost souls of patients. On the other hand, a classic example where a river system offers a link between the three worlds is provided by the religious frameworks of the Evenks, whose cosmology is characteristic of the Tungus-Manchu peoples of Siberia.

EVENK COSMOLOGY – A SPECIAL CASE

The Evenks conceive of a universe consisting of the three characteristic levels identified by Eliade. This consists of the upper world called ugu buga, associated with the sky; the middle world called dulugu buga, where mankind dwells; and the lower world named kherguergu buga, which is the domain of deceased kinsmen and the spirits of illness. Linking all of these three worlds and providing the counterpart of the Cosmic Tree is the mythical Clan River whose headwaters originate in the upper world and which in turn flows through to an underground sea extending to the furthest reaches of the lower world.[4]

The upper world, to all intents and purposes, resembles the familiar world of everyday reality, but on a grander scale – the gods and spirits who dwell here are prototypes for man below. For example, ugu buga is the realm of the creator god Amaka, a very old man dressed in luxuriant fur clothing, who in earliest times taught humans how to use fire and tools, and how to domesticate reindeer. It is also the dwelling place of Eksheri, considered the master of animals, birds and fish, who holds the 'threads' of their destiny in his hands, dictating when they live or die. Eksheri was very much a being to whom the shaman would appeal regarding the overall success of the hunt, for if Eksheri was not propitiated he could direct his spirit-rulers to drive the animals away in different directions. Eksheri also represents the 'heavenly' counterpart of the Clan Mistress of the lower world, whom we shall meet later as the guardian of animal souls sought for the hunt.

Also residing in ugu buga is the thunder-god Agdy, who upon awakening gives vent to peals of thunder and flashes of lightning which destroy evil spirits. Here too lives the old man Dylacha, who, as the master of heat and light, toils unceasingly to provide warmth for mankind – an effort very much appreciated during the Siberian winter. It is he who lights the heavenly fire, collects its heat in his huge leather bag, and then, when the spring comes, disperses it to middle earth with the assistance of his sons, helping to warm the land and melt the icy rivers.

All of these beings, as one would expect, are considered benevolent, but this is not the case with the dwellers in the lower world, who are much more formidable. In *khergu-ergu buga* the world is turned on its heels so that what has been living becomes dead, and what was dead comes alive. It is a domain that on one particular level, called *buni*, is inhabited by dead clansmen whose bodies are cold and who live there without breathing, but who nevertheless continue to hunt and fish like the living. However, *khergu-ergu buga* is also the realm of the spirits of illness and disease, and of the Clan Mistress who watches for breaches of tribal taboos. The rulers of the lower world, known collectively as the *khargi*, cannot be ignored for they govern the ancestor-spirits and must be respected as overlords of the dead. The Evenks say that the *khargi*, including the Clan Mistress who rules the hunt, are themselves half-animal and half-human, so ironically, despite the dangers, the lower world provides the possibility for totemic clan unity. The shaman is special because he has a sacred link with the totem animal, can conquer the domain of death, and is then 'reborn', alive, into the familiar world of middle earth.

The unique role of the shaman is sometimes represented in hero myths. The Evenks have a legend about a figure called Main, who is a master of destiny, a hunter in the heavens, and an archetypal cosmic shaman. One day Kheglen, the heavenly elk, stole the sun from the sky by impaling it on its antlers. This plunged the world into seemingly eternal night and humankind was at a loss what to do. Main, the hero shaman, then came forth, donning his skis and heading off to the opening in the heavenly vault. Once in *ugu buga*, Main was able to track down the elk and strike it with an arrow from his bow. He thus was able to return the sun – and all its light and warmth – to Middle Earth, while in turn becoming recognised as a guardian of life itself.

However, if a shaman like Main has to learn to be effective in the upper world – and in the above myth he is really a counterpart of Dylacha, the god of warmth – he also has to negotiate with the special figure of the Clan Mistress, *bugady-eninintyn*, who dwells in the lower world. Having announced in a song that he will confirm how many animals can be caught in the hunt, he journeys through a whirlpool and along a river to the subterranean clan territories, overcomes various obstacles in his path, and meets the Clan Mistress face to face. She appears before him in a forbidding form that is half-animal and half-human but undaunted by her appearance he knows he must persuade her to release the animal souls under her command. Finally, after pleading with her at length, he is granted permission to capture a certain number of animals – these he turns into silken threads and hides inside his shaman drum. When he returns to middle earth he takes his drum to the clan's hunting grounds and shakes the threads forth. They then transform into real animals which will provide the future catch for his fellow hunters.

Nevertheless, if appeasing the gods of both the upper and lower worlds is the central task of the shaman, he does not always act alone. Often he is accompanied by helper guides who assist him in wending his way from one realm to the next, and invariably he has various allies – spirits or familiars – which can help him perform his task successfully.

SPIRIT GUIDES

In the shaman's world, spirit allies have many functions – they can detect the origins of illness, be despatched to recover lost souls, be summoned in acts of aggression and show a clear path past obstacles which might arise on the shaman's spirit quest. As we have already seen, spirit helpers may appear to shamans in dreams, in visions, and spontaneously after initiations. In some societies shamans also exchange or inherit them. In all cases, however, spirit guides are perceived as crucial to the shaman's resolve and power – literal embodiments of his psychic and magical strength.

There are two basic types of spirit guide. Firstly there are spirits which are substantially under the shaman's control and which serve as his familiars. But there are also other spirits – thought of more as guardians or helpers – who are available when he needs to call on their aid. These may be minor deities or the spirits of deceased shamans: entities who maintain a certain independence in their particular realm and who are not automatically subject to the control of the shaman.

Siberian shamans generally have animal familiars like bears, wolves and hares, or birds like geese, eagles or owls. Yakuts, for example, view bulls, eagles and bears as their strongest allies,

Shaman spirit-guides (drawing by Martin Carey)
The Woodstock Aquarian

preferring them to wolves or dogs – the spirits of lesser shamans. The
Barama Carib, meanwhile, associates different classes of spirits with
different types of pebble which he places in his shaman-rattle: these
he can summon at will.

The guardian spirit is on a different level, however. The example in
Chapter 2, of Tamang shamanism in Nepal, provides this distinction.
Here Bhirendra was guided by the spirit of his dead grandfather,
and it was through him, as well as through the tutelage of his father,
that he was able to acquire shamanic visionary consciousness.

On occasion, as Mircea Eliade has pointed out, the guardian
spirit also becomes a type of *alter ego* of the shaman – his psychic
counterpart on the inner planes. To this extent we can understand
the magical claims of human-animal transformation, for on these
occasions the shaman projects his consciousness into an animal

28

form on an imaginal level and it is in this 'body' that he goes forth on his spirit-journey. Chukchee and Eskimo shamans maintain that they can change themselves into wolves, while Lapps can become bears or reindeers. The Semang shamans of the Malay Peninsula, on the other hand, believe they can transform themselves into tigers. Not that this type of magical transformation is without its dangers however. Sometimes shamans fight each other on the inner planes in their magical bodies. If a shaman 'dies' during this encounter, it is often said that he will die in real life as well, for his 'essence' will have been destroyed.

On the more basic level of animal familiars, a good example of their role is provided by the Netsilik Eskimos of the Arctic coast of Canada. Here established shamans, or *angatkoks,* recruit young prospective male shamans and put them through a magical apprenticeship. They join the household of a shaman-teacher, are instructed in observing ritual taboos, and then move to a special igloo where they learn shamanic techniques. The teacher provides his novice with a *tunraq* – a helper spirit, or familiar – and in the beginning it is clear that the *tunraq* has more power than its new owner. However, with time the young Eskimo shaman will learn to tame it. As the shaman grows in experience and confidence he may later acquire further *tunraqs* and can keep doing so throughout his life. The famous shaman Iksivalitaq, whom anthropologist Asen Balikci calls 'the last Netsilik shaman of importance', and who was still alive in the 1940s, had seven *tunraqs* – including the spirit of Big Mountain, the ghosts of three dead men, one of them his grandfather, and the spirits of a sea scorpion, a killer whale and a black dog without ears.

According to Asen Balikci, who studied Netsilik culture in some detail, *tunraqs* like to be 'frequently called and used', thus reinforcing the notion that ideally there should be a strong personal bond between the shaman and his helper spirits. But it is also possible for *tunraqs* to unleash their potency against their owners if things go wrong. Perhaps a shaman has sent his *tunraq* on a difficult mission and the spirit has failed to achieve its task. It can then become a 'reversed spirit' or *tunraq kigdloretto* – angry, bloodthirsty and out of control – wreaking havoc on its former owner and relatives, and bringing with it sickness and death.

Even at the best of times in Netsilik Eskimo society *tunraqs* have an uneasy relationship with their irascible owners. Balikci quotes two cases where aggressive shamanising was the result of jealous rivalry:

> Kaormik was a better bear hunter than Amaoligardjuk's son, so Amaoli-
> gardjuk, a shaman, became jealous and sent his *tunraq* polar bear
> against Kaormik. The bear scratched the left side of his face severely but
> failed to kill him. Amaoligardjuk added after: 'This man is hard to kill!'

And, on another occasion,

> Tavoq, a shaman, grew jealous of Angutitak, an excellent hunter,
> and scolded him repeatedly. Angutitak, a quiet and fearful man, never
> answered, until one day he accused Tavoq of being a mediocre and
> lazy hunter. Tavoq avenged himself by dispatching his *tunraq* to raise a
> snow storm just at the moment when Angutitak was stalking caribou.[5]

Another remarkable instance of the sometimes precarious relationship between a shaman and his spirit guide is provided by an
unnamed Goldi shaman who had lengthy discussions with Russian
anthropologist Lev Shternberg in the early 1900s. He explained to
Shternberg that he had been drawn to shamanism initially by having
bad headaches which other shamans were unable to cure, and he
yearned to be a shaman himself.

One night while he was asleep in his bed he was visited by a very
beautiful woman who resembled other Goldi women but was much
smaller (around 70 cm in height). She told him that she was one of
his spirit ancestors – *ayami* – and had taught shamanic healing to other
shamans. Now she was going to teach him.

The *ayami* also said that she would now regard the man as her
husband and would provide him with assistant spirits that could
help him to heal. She was also somewhat threatening. 'If you will
not obey . . .' she told him sternly, 'so much the worse for you.
I shall kill you.'[6]

The shaman related to Shternberg how his spirit wife could change
form at will – sometimes appearing like an old woman, sometimes as
a wolf or winged tiger – and that she had taken him on aerial journeys
to other locations. She had likewise bequeathed him three assistant
familiar spirits – a panther, bear and tiger – to help out during his
shamanising. It was they who provided the source of his shamanic
power: 'When I am [shamanising] the *ayami* and the assistant spirits
are possessing me,' he told Shternberg; '. . . whether big or small, they
penetrate me, as smoke or vapour would. When the *ayami* is within me,
it is she who speaks through my mouth.'[7]

We see here a blurring of the distinction made earlier between
shamans and mediums – in a sense this shaman has become possessed
by his spirit guides. However, it is really a case of the shaman

consciously tapping his inner resources – in this case his multiple spirit helpers – to perform the act of magical healing. To this extent he is still exercising his will, rather than responding passively to the situation and channelling an unknown force from realms beyond his mind.

Overall, as we have said, the relationship between the shaman and his allies is a vital but sometimes precarious one, and the latter may, for a time, dictate the state of play. The relationship may on occasions take the form of a spiritual 'marriage' – as in the Goldi case above – or else it might involve the shaman honouring his helper spirits through song, dance and ritual. It might entail making offerings to fetishes linked to his spirit guides, actively respecting taboos (for example, not eating the meat of the animal concerned) or simply agreeing to keep the existence of the spirit ally a secret from others. Whatever the situation, it is clear that in the final analysis the shaman depends very much on his helper spirits, whether they are animal familiars under his control or cosmic denizens who hold the key to realms beyond, in the upper and lower worlds. The shaman's unique role, after all, is as an *intermediary*: he is special because he is effective on more than one plane of reality and it is up to him to maintain that special access by mustering *all* the assistance he can obtain.

4 • RITUALS AND THE INNER WORLD

Ceremonial ritual is the outer enactment of an internal event. In all religions, and also in shamanism and ceremonial magic, those performing a ritual believe that what they are doing is not simply theatrical but accords with some sort of sacred, inner reality – that for a time they are caught up in a mystical drama, perhaps involving union with a god, identification with a source of spiritual healing or the act of embodying some sort of transcendent power. In such a way the shaman, priest or magician believes he is tapping into a dimension which is much larger and more awesome than the world of familiar reality. It is very much a case of participating in a *mystery* – of leaving the everyday realm and, for a sacred and special period of time, entering the Cosmos.

Many anthropologists and sociologists have a problem with this. Because they are trained to record external events in detail, to monitor behaviour patterns and the ways in which such behaviour proves meaningful in the social matrix, they are often inclined to believe that that is *all* that is happening.

Shamanism is no exception. To many observers the shaman is little more than an exotic performer, a person who, through evocative and stimulating ritual is able to induce a state of hysteria which deludes both himself and his audience.

32

A Blackfoot Indian shaman wearing animal costumes (Early 19th century)

A case in point is provided by Weston La Barre's commentary on shamanism in his epic work on the origins of religion, *The Ghost Dance*. La Barre makes the valid point that from earliest times shamans learned to imitate the movements and sounds of birds and animals. This was natural because animal shamans would wish to identify with forces in the underworld responsible for the success of the hunt, while bird shamans would wish to identify with spirits of the weather and the sky. Noting that the Yakuts of Siberia, for example, are skilled in imitating the calls of such birds as the lapwing, falcon, eagle and cuckoo, he emphasises that

> . . . to become like animals and birds, one must not only dress in their skins and masks but also imitate their behaviours. In addition to birds' mastery of the air, which shamans achieve in trance and in their flying dreams, the major attribute of birds is their song . . . bird shamans [borrow] song from their sources of power.[1]

However, when it comes to the crunch, La Barre, like other anthropologists concerned primarily with social explanations, is inclined to view the shaman simply as an imitator and manipulator, and his ritual as a deception. He quotes Diamond Jenness's description of a Copper Eskimo shamanic ritual observed in the 1920's:

> The shaman is not conscious of acting a part: he becomes in his own mind the animal or the shade of the dead man who is deemed to possess him. To the audience, too, this strange figure, with its wild and frenzied appearance, its ventriloquistic cries and its unearthly falsetto gabble, with only a broken word here and there of intelligible speech, is no longer a human being, but the thing it personifies. Their minds become receptive to the wildest imaginings, and they see the strangest and most fantastic happenings.[2]

La Barre, who follows this quote with the observation that 'the resemblance to stage illusion is striking', also emphasises that shamans can often be downright dishonest in their rituals, and recalls the case of the Kiowa shaman Lone Bear, who was so 'incompetent' that the ethnographer watching him, William Bascom, could see him fumble red clay from his pouch and chew it in his mouth – later spitting it out as his own 'blood'.

But is this interpretation a 'true' representation of what really took place? Whether this particular deception occurred or not, in general what seems more likely is that on such occasions the shaman is resorting to ceremonial activities, and using ritual objects, which on a physical level reflect his inner, psychic processes. If we consider rituals in this light, it is quite reasonable that red clay *can* become blood and that the Kirghiz shaman who imitates the sound of birds' wings experiences the sensation of actually flying.

This is a conclusion also reached by American anthropologist Michael Harner, in evaluating the dance of the Beast Gods as performed by the Zuni Pueblo:

> The Beast Gods are summoned by dancing, rattling and drumming, and the dancers work themselves into a frenzied condition in which they

imitate the actions and cries of animals. Those dancers assuming the personality of the bear may even wear actual bear paws over their hands. But this dance of the Beast Gods is more than simple imitation, since the Zuni dancer, like a North American Plains Indian doing an Eagle or Buffalo Dance, is striving to go beyond imitation to become one with the animal . . . Likewise, a Zuni dancer wearing the mask of one of the *kachina* gods is doing more than impersonating the *kachina*. Transported into an altered state of consciousness by the dancing, drumming, rattling and whirr of bull roarers he 'becomes for the time being the actual embodiment of the spirit which is believed to reside in the mask'.[3]

Another example of the transformatory nature of ritual is provided by the Australian Aborigines of Forrest River, who undertake ceremonial initiations which feature the symbolic death and resurrection of the candidate and his ascent to the sky:

The usual method is as follows: The master assumes the form of a skeleton and equips himself with a small bag, in which he puts the candidate, whom his magic has reduced to the size of an infant. Then seating himself astride the Rainbow-Serpent, he begins to pull himself up by his arms, as if climbing a rope. When near the top, he throws the candidate into the sky, 'killing' him. Once they are in the sky, the master inserts into the candidate's body small rainbow-serpents, *brimures* [i.e. small fresh-water snakes], and quartz crystals (which have the same name as the mythical Rainbow-Serpent). After this operation the candidate is brought back to earth, still on the Rainbow-Serpent's back. The master again introduces magical objects into his body, this time through the navel, and wakens him by touching him with a magical stone. The candidate returns to normal size. On the following day the ascent by the Rainbow-Serpent is repeated in the same way.[4]

Clearly in such rituals there are physical observances – that one can actually see externally – and symbolic, mythic processes that are represented by the ceremonial sequence of events. Unlike the scientifically trained Western observer, who no doubt would miss much of the import of such a ritual as that described above, the shaman does not distinguish between 'real' and 'unreal' worlds. The entire magical domain explored during the shamanising is an integrated expression of both 'natural' and 'magical' events, for the shaman is 'breaking through in plane' from the everyday reality to the upper or lower worlds. For him, in a nutshell, the magic is real.

When we look at shamanic costumes we also see evidence of the mythic processes involved. The Japanese shamans observed by Carmen Blacker wore a cap of eagle and owl feathers and cloaks adorned with stuffed snakes, intended to facilitate 'the passage from one world to another'. Emphasising this point, Blacker notes that '. . . the magic clothes and instruments, of which the drum is the most important, embody in their shape, in the materials of which they are made, in the patterns and figures engraved upon them, symbolic links with the other world.'[5]

Likewise, Yakut shamans wear a kaftan decorated with a solar disc – representing the opening of the underworld – while the Goldi dons a coat depicting the Cosmic Tree and 'power animals' like bears and wild cats, which are part of his mythic experience. Teleut shamans often wear winged owl caps to symbolise magical flight, while the Buryat shaman costume is heavily laden with iron ornaments which portray the iron bones of immortality. The bears, leopards, serpents and lizards which appear on it are the shaman's helping spirits.

To some extent, then, one is obliged to heed the shaman's own perceptions of his universe, expressed in his own terms. For many anthropologists, especially those not attuned to the mind-set of the shaman this is especially difficult. However, the apparently formidable gap between scientific anthropology and mythic experiential shamanism is capable of being narrowed. More psychologists are now taking note of such phenomena as near-death and out-of-the-body experiences which strongly suggest that consciousness can operate functionally at a distance from the body. Here, ordinary citizens in an urban Western environment report aerial sensations not so far removed from the shamanic experience. The following descriptions from Winnebago shaman Thunder Cloud are much more believable than they first seem, when considered in this context.

Thunder Cloud was a member of the Medicine Dance Secret Society and a highly respected shaman. He maintained that he was able to consciously recall two previous incarnations, in the second actually watching the people burying him after his death. He then journeyed towards the Setting Sun, arriving at a village where there were other dead people:

> I was told that I would have to stop there for four nights, but, in reality, I stayed there for four years. The people enjoy themselves here. They have all sorts of dances of a lively kind. From that place we went up to where Earthmaker lives and I saw him and talked to him, face to face, even as I am talking to you now. I saw the spirits too and, indeed, I was like one of them.
>
> Thence I came to this earth for the third time and here I am. I am going through the same that I knew before.[6]

One can only conclude that the world of the shaman, bizarre as it must sometimes seem to outsiders, is nevertheless totally real to the person experiencing it. Thunder Cloud also describes shamanic dancing and healing from the view of the spirit-vision associated with it:

> at Blue Clay Bank [St Paul] there lives one who is a dancing grizzly-bear spirit. Whenever I am in great trouble I was to pour tobacco, as much as I thought necessary, and he would help me. This grizzly bear gave me songs and the power of beholding a holy thing: he gave me his claws, claws that are holy. Then the grizzly bear danced and performed while he danced. He tore his abdomen open and, making himself holy, healed himself again. This he repeated. One grizzly bear shot claws at the other and the wounded one became badly choked with blood. Then both made themselves holy again and cured themselves.[7]

Clearly, in this instance Thunder Cloud is speaking both literally and metaphysically. Although the grizzly-bear spirit is associated with a specific location (Blue Clay Bank), the descriptions provided are of magical events – Thunder Cloud has seen the miraculous healing not on a physical level but in his spirit-vision. Nevertheless, the two levels of perception have begun to merge. The demonstration of healing has provided what the shaman himself calls 'holy' revelations. The shamanising is occurring in sacred space.

Having explored aspects of the shaman's experiential realm we should now also consider two of the specifics of shamanic technique – the shaman's drum and his use of song. Both are of central importance since they offer a means of entering the shamanic state of consciousness and attracting helper spirits. Without skills of this sort, a shaman can hardly hope to be successful.

THE SHAMAN'S DRUM

The drum has a special role in shamanism for it is literally the vehicle that 'carries' the shaman to the other world. Often it is closely identified with a horse, or some other sort of animal. Soyots call their shaman drums *khamu-at*, meaning 'shaman horse' and Altaic shamans embellish their drums with horse symbols. Interestingly, the anthropologist L. P. Potapov discovered that the Altaians people name their drum not after the animals whose skin is used in manufacture (camel or dappled horse) but after the domestic horses actually used as steeds. This confirms the idea that the drum is a mode of transport: it is the monotonous rhythm of the drum which the shaman 'rides' into the upper and lower worlds. A Soyot poem also makes this clear:

The drum is central to shamanism. This engraving is from Noord en Oost Tartarye Holland, 1705 and shows a Tungus shaman from Siberia

Skin-coverd drum,
Fulfil my wishes,
Like flitting clouds, carry me
Through the lands of dusk
And below the leaden sky,
Sweep along like wind
Over the mountain peaks![8]

The sound of the drum acts as a focusing device for the shaman. It creates an atmosphere of concentration and resolve, enabling him to sink deep into trance as he shifts his attention to the inner journey of the spirit.

It is not uncommon, either, for the drum to have a symbolic link with the Centre of the World, or the World Tree. The Evenks fashion the rims of their drums from the wood of the sacred larch, and Lapp shamans decorate their drums with mythic symbols like the Cosmic Tree, the sun, moon or rainbow.[9]

So, the two crucial points which emerge from this are that the shaman's drum not only produces an altered state of consciousness, but confirms the shift in perception, which results from the drumming, as the basis for a mythic encounter.

Recent research among the Salish Indians, undertaken by Wolfgang G. Jilek, found that rhythmic shamanic drumming produced a drumbeat frequency in the theta wave EEG frequency (4–7 cycles/second) – the brainwave range associated with dreams, hypnotic imagery and trance.[10] This is hardly surprising, for shamanism is a type of mythic 'lucid dreaming'. In the latter category of dreaming one is 'aware' that one is dreaming and likewise, in shamanism, one is conscious in the altered state and able to act purposefully within it. Shamans invariably report their encounters not as hallucinations or fanciful imagination but as experientially valid: what happens during the spirit-journey is *real* in that dimension.

SHAMAN SONG

Song is another vital aspect of shamanism. It is through songs and chants that the shaman expresses both his power and his intent. Songs are the sounds of the gods and spirits and, like the sacred drum, can help the shaman feel propelled by their energy. As the Apache shaman-chief Geronimo once proclaimed: 'As I sing, I go through the air to a holy place where Yusun [the Supreme Being] will give me power to do wonderful things. I am surrounded by little clouds, and as I go through the air I change, becoming spirit only.'[11]

The Australian Aborigines also provide an excellent example of the link between musical sounds and the gods. Some Aborigines, for example, believe that their creator gods dwell in bull-roarers which may be whirled in the air to restore energy and vibrancy to both tribe and totem. They also believe that the songs they continue to sing today are the same as those sung by their ancestors in the Dreamtime, when the gods brought the world into being. The most sacred songs are chanted at the special sites where the gods were thought to roam: these songs are considered to have a special magic which helps to produce abundant food and water supplies.

When the explorers Baldwin Spencer and F. J. Gillen visited the Warraminga Aborigines and neighbouring tribes in 1901 they saw a marvellous fire ceremony where torches five metres long blazed to the wild music of the *Kingilli* singers. They listened to legends about Wollungua, the great serpent whose head reached up to the sky, and when visiting the Kaitish Aborigines observed a rain-making ceremony which included imitations of the plover-call.

The Central Australian Ljaba Aranda Aborigines, meanwhile, have a Honey-Ant Song which describes the insects nestling under the roots of native mulga trees. But these honey-ants are also thought to be ancestor spirits with elaborate decorations on their bodies. When the song is sung, the Aborigines performing the ceremony sweep brushes of mulga over themselves, allowing the honey-ant spirits to come forth – for they believe themselves to be magically possessed at this time by the ancestors. Such a song is typical of the sacred music which links Aborigines of the Dreamtime to their forefathers.[12]

Sometimes, as a bridge to sacred reality, song may also be evoked from the shaman's own being. Anthropologist Joan Halifax writes:

> As the World Tree stands at the centre of the vast planes of the cosmos, song stands at the intimate centre of the cosmos of the individual. At that moment when the shaman song emerges, when the sacred breath rises up from the depths of the heart, the centre is found, and the source of all that is divine has been tapped.[13]

A wonderful description of this process is provided by the North American Gitksan Indian, Isaac Tens. At the age of 30, Tens began to fall continually into trance states and experienced dramatic, and often terrifying, visions. On one occasion animal spirits and snake-like trees seemed to be chasing him and an owl took hold of him, catching his face and trying to lift him up. Later, while Tens was on a hunting trip, an owl appeared to him again, high up in a cedar tree. Tens shot the owl and went to retrieve it in the bushes, but found to his amazement that it had disappeared. He then hastened back towards his village, puzzled and alarmed, but on the way again fell into a trance:

> When I came to, my head was buried in a snowbank. I got up and walked on the ice up the river to the village. There I met my father who had just come out to look for me, for he had missed me. We went back together to my house. Then my heart started to beat fast, and I began to tremble, just as had happened a while before, when the *halaaits* (medicine-men) were trying to fix me up. My flesh seemed to be boiling . . . my body was quivering. While I remained in this state, I began to sing. A chant was coming out of me without my being able

to do anything to stop it. Many things appeared to me presently: huge birds and other animals. They were calling me. I saw a *meskyawawderh* [a kind of bird] and a *mesqagweeuk* [bullhead fish]. These were visible only to me, not to the others in my house. Such visions happen when a man is about to become a *halaait*; they occur of their own accord. The songs force themselves out, complete, without any attempt to compose them. But I learned and memorised these songs by repeating them.[14]

While such visions may seem to belong solely to the exotic world of the primitive shaman, it is interesting that urban Westerners who find themselves in a shamanic context sometimes report comparable initiations. An impressive account is provided by the distinguished American anthropologist Michael Harner, formerly an Associate Professor at the New School for Social Research, New York. In 1959, Harner was invited by the American Museum of Natural History to study the Conibo Indians of the Peruvian Amazon. He set off the following year for the Ucayali River and found the Indians friendly and receptive on his arrival. Harner, however, wished to be more than an anthropologist: he hoped to be initiated as a shaman. He was told that to tap the magical reality he would have to drink the sacred potion *ayahuasca*, made from the Banisteriopsis vine. *Ayahuasca* contains the alkaloids harmine and harmaline and produces out-of-the-body experiences, telepathic and psychic impressions and spectacular visions. Among the Conibo the sacred drink was also known as 'the little death' and its powers were regarded with awe.

Harner took the shamanic potion at night, accompanied by an elder of the village. Soon the sound of a waterfall filled his ears and his body became numb. As he began to hallucinate he became aware of a giant crocodile, from whose jaws rushed a torrent of water. These waters formed an ocean and Harner saw a dragon-headed ship sailing towards him. Several hundred oars propelled the vessel, producing a rhythmic, swishing sound as it moved along. Harner now experienced the music of the inner worlds:

> I became conscious . . . of the most beautiful singing I have ever heard in my life, high-pitched and ethereal, emanating from myriad voices on board the galley. As I looked more closely at the deck, I could make out large numbers of people with the heads of blue jays and the bodies of humans, not unlike the bird-headed gods of ancient Egyptian tomb paintings. At the same time, some energy-essence began to float from my chest up into the boat.[15]

Harner's mind now seemed to function on several levels as he was granted sacred visions by the spirit creatures – secrets, they told him, which would normally be given only to those about to die. These visions included a survey of the birth of the earth, aeons before the advent of man, and an explanation of how human consciousness had evolved.

In traditional shamanism, irrespective of its cultural context, it is not uncommon for the shaman to be shown by the gods how society came into existence, how the worlds were formed, and how man has a privileged and special relationship with the gods. What is so interesting about Michael Harner's account is that he was able to enter the shaman's exotic world so totally, despite his Western intellectual background.

5 • SACRED PLANTS

Sacred plants – plants which cause visions and hallucinations – are a central feature of shamanism in many regions of the world. To modern urban Westerners the idea of visions induced by psychotropic means may seem like an aberration, perhaps even a type of decadence. Indeed, during the late 1960s, when the youthful exploration of psychedelics was rampant, one would often read in the press about mystical episodes being 'artificially' produced by drugs like LSD and psilocybin. The perception was that such drugs invariably produced a distortion, a wavering from 'reality'.

In the pre-literate world of the shaman the exact opposite is true. Here the sacred plants are believed to open the doors to the heavens, to allow contact with the gods and spirits, and to permit access to a greater reality beyond. The Jivaro of Ecuador, for example, describe the familiar world as 'a lie'. There is only one reality – the world of the supernatural.

Our attitude to such matters in modern Western society is mirrored by our language. The word 'drug' itself is a highly coloured term and is frequently associated with acts that are disapproved of in the mainstream. As a consequence the 'drug experience', if one could call it that, is not something valued by modern Western culture as a whole. Little distinction exists in the popular mind between sacred or psychedelic drugs, like those which feature in shamanism, and the recreational, addictive or analgesic drugs which are part of contemporary urban life.

Sacred plants – a doorway to mythic visions (drawing by Martin Carey)
Aquarian Angel

A revealing anecdote which throws light on modern attitudes from a shamanic point of view is provided by anthropologist Peter Furst in his book *Hallucinogens and Culture*. Furst was present when a newspaper reporter referred to peyote as a 'drug' in front of a Huichol shaman. The shaman replied succinctly: 'Aspirina is a drug, peyote is sacred.'[1]

Hallucinogenic plants of the type used in shamanism thus require some sort of clarification. While by definition such plants are toxic – if we mean by that something which has a distinct biodynamic effect on the body – this does not mean that such plants are invariably poisonous, though some are in certain dosages (e.g. *Datura* or *Sophora secundiflora*). As far as we know, none of the hallucinogenic plants utilised in shamanism is addictive. Also it is important that we make the distinction that these plants do not simply modify moods but are capable of producing a dramatic and often profound change in perception. Colours are enhanced, spirits may appear, the sacramental plant appears god-like to the shaman who has invoked it ceremonially, and perhaps a cosmic bridge or smoke tunnel appears in the shaman's vision, allowing him to ascend to the heavens. In every way the sacred plant is a doorway to a realm that is awesome and wondrous, and the undertaking is not one which is taken lightly. To this extent, then, the ritual use of hallucinogenic plants is not recreational but *transformative* – one undertakes the vision-quest to 'learn' or to 'see', not to 'escape' into a world of 'fantasy'.

Psychologists have produced various terms to describe the substances which produce such radical shifts in consciousness. Dr Humphry Osmond, an English psychiatrist, coined the term *psychedelic* meaning 'mind-revealing' or 'mind-manifesting' but a term preferred by many is *psychotomimetic*: substances within this category are capable of inducing temporary psychotic states of such intensity that the 'visionary' or 'dream' world appears profoundly real. In shamanic societies experiences like this are highly valued. Sacred plants remove the barriers between humankind and the realm of gods and spirits, and from them one receives wisdom and learning. The gods *know*; the sacred plant *speaks*.

Generally, the psychotropic components of sacred plants are contained in the alkaloids, resins, glucosides and essential oils found in the leaves, bark, stem, flowers, sap, roots or seeds of the plants. The regions richest in naturally occurring hallucinogenic plants are Mexico and South America. On the other hand, with the exception of *Amanita muscaria* (apparently deified by the Aryans of Vedic India as the god Soma), datura and marijuana, Asia is comparatively lacking in such plant species. And they appear not to be used shamanically to any great extent in Africa and Australasia.

In Mexico the most important plants in shamanic usage are peyote, psilocybe mushrooms and morning glory, while in South America the most prevalent hallucinogen is a drink made from the Banisteriopsis vine, and known variously as *ayahuasca*, *caapi*, *natema* or *yaje*. Other plant species used in that region are San Pedro cactus, native tobacco, the brugmansias, a hallucinogenic snuff known as *yopo*, and virola.

The use of such plants extends back for hundreds, and in some cases many thousands, of years. Peyote, for example, was known to the Toltecs some 1,900 years prior to the arrival of the Europeans, while the ritual use of San Pedro cactus – established through its association with jaguar motifs and spirit beings on ceremonial pottery – seems to date back at least 3,000 years. The ritual use of psychotropic mushrooms in Mexico certainly pre-dates the Conquests by many centuries – as evidenced by surviving Mayan 'mushroom stones' – while an Aztec mural at Teotihuacan depicting a Mother Goddess who personifies the Morning Glory or *ololiuhqui* – sacred to the Aztecs – dates from c.500.

PEYOTE

Deriving its name from the Aztec *peyotl*, the famous peyote cactus (*Lophophora williamsii*) was the first hallucinogenic plant discovered by the Europeans in the Americas. It is associated primarily with the Huichol Indians of the Sierra Madre in Mexico, although it is also used by the Cora and Tarahumara Indians, the Amerindian Kiowa and Comanche, and in the more recently established Native American Church which now has around 250,000 members.

Peyote is a complex hallucinogenic plant capable of producing a wide range of effects. Its main alkaloid constituent is mescaline but it also contains around thirty other psychoactive agents. Users may experience vividly coloured images, shimmering auras around objects, feelings of weightlessness and also unusual auditory and tactile sensations.

The first detailed description of the cactus was provided by Dr Francisco Hernandez, physician to King Philip II of Spain, who studied Aztec medicine quite thoroughly. He writes:

> The root is of nearly medium size, sending forth no branches or leaves above the ground, but with a certain woolliness adhering to it on account of which it could not aptly be figured by me. Both men and women are said to be harmed by it. It appears to be of a sweetish taste and moderately hot. Ground up and applied to painful joints, it is said to give relief. Wonderful properties are attributed to this root, if any faith can be given to what is commonly said among them on this point. It causes those devouring it to be able to foresee and predict things.[2]

Not surprisingly, the cactus was fiercely suppressed in Mexico by Christian missionaries because of its 'pagan' associations. A priest, Padre Nicholas de Leon, asked potential converts to Christianity:

> Art thou a soothsayer? Dost thou foretell events by reading omens, interpreting dreams or by tracing circles and figures on water? Dost thou garnish with flower garlands the places where idols are kept? Dost thou suck the blood of others? Dost thou wander about at night,

calling upon demons to help thee? Hast thou drunk Peyote or given it to others to drink, in order to discover secrets or to discover where stolen or lost articles were?[3]

Fortunately the Huichol Indians managed to escape the proselytising influence of the Christian missionaries even though the Sierra Madre came under Spanish influence in 1722. Today the Indians continue to regard the peyote cactus as divine, associating the region where it grows with Paradise (*Wirikuta*) and the plant itself with the Divine Deer, or Master of the Deer species.

Peyote cactus

47

Each year groups of Huichols – usually numbering 10–15 people – make a pilgrimage to gather the peyote, which they call *Hikuri*. They are led by a shaman who is in contact with Tatewari, the peyote god: Tatewari is the archetypal 'first shaman' who led the first peyote pilgrimage and subsequent shamans seek to emulate his example.

The distance between the Sierra Madre and the high desert of San Luis Potosi where the cactus grows, is around 300 miles, and although in the past this pilgrimage was always undertaken on foot, it is now considered permissible to travel by car, bus or train providing offerings, prayers and acts of ritual cleansing are made *en route*. The desert destination, Wirikuta, is regarded as the 'mythic place of Origin' of the Huichols. As Peter Furst notes:

> The pattern was established long ago, in mythic times, when the Great Shaman, Fire, addressed as Tatewari, Our Grandfather, led the ancestral gods on the first peyote quest. It is told that the fire god came upon them as they sat in a circle in the Huichol temple, each complaining of a different ailment. Asked to divine the cause of their ills, the Great Shaman, Fire, said they were suffering because they had not gone to hunt the divine Deer [Peyote] in Wirikuta, as their own ancestors had done, and so had been deprived of the healing powers of its miraculous flesh. It was decided to take up bow and arrow and to follow Tatewari to 'find their lives' in the distant land of the Deer-Peyote.[4]

At Wirikuta dwell the divine ancestors, Kakauyarixi, and the Divine Deer, personified by the sacred cactus of the region, is believed to represent life itself. When the shaman leading the pilgrimage finds the peyote he declares that he has 'seen the deer tracks'. He then 'shoots' the cactus with his bow and arrow as if it were a deer pursued in the hunt.

The peyote cactus is subsequently collected and shared out to those participating in the pilgrimage. The cactus is either consumed direct in small pieces, or macerated and mixed with water (symbolising the dry and wet seasons). Huichols say the sacred Deer is a mount to the upper levels of the Cosmos and a spirit helper who can be called upon during healing ceremonies.

A Western observer, Prem Das, who now runs a shamanic study centre in California, has described the feelings which come from partaking of peyote with the Huichols:

> When I looked down to the ground I saw peyote cacti everywhere about me, and they seemed to glow with a special luminescence of

their own. The two richly embroidered Huichol peyote bags I was wearing were easily filled and held at least a hundred peyote cacti of various sizes. I ate several more, continuing to watch the luminous and constantly changing cloud formations in the awesome and penetrating silence of Wirikuta.

I began to cry as I thought of my own people, my own race, with its atomic bombs and missiles sitting ready to destroy everyone and everything at any moment. Why, I wondered, why had we become so isolated and estranged from the harmony and beauty of our wonderful planet?

I heard an answer that seemed to come from all around me, and it rose in my mind's eye like a great time-lapse vision. I saw a human being rise from the earth, stand for a moment, and then dissolve back into it. It was only a brief moment, and in that moment our whole lives passed. Then I saw a huge city rise out of the desert floor beneath me, exist for a second, and then vanish back into the vastness of the desert. The plants, rocks, and the earth under me were saying, 'Yes, this is how it really is, your life, the city you live in.' It was as if in my peyotized state I was able to perceive and communicate with a resonance or vibration that surrounded me. Those inner barriers which defined 'me' as a separate identity from 'that' – my environment – had dissolved. An overwhelming realisation poured through me – that the human race and all technology formed by it are nothing other than flowers of the earth. The painful problem that had confronted me disappeared entirely, to be replaced with a vision of people and their technology as temporary forms through which Mother Earth was expressing herself. I felt a surge of happiness and ecstasy which flowed out to dance with all forms of the earth about me; I cried with joy and thanked Wirikuta, don José and the Huichols for such a profound blessing.[5]

PSILOCYBE MUSHROOMS

For a long time, the existence of the 'sacred mushrooms' of Mexico was doubted by expert botanists. In 1915 William Safford had addressed the Botanical Society in Washington, arguing that sacred inebriating mushrooms did not exist – they had been confused with peyote. It took Richard Evans Schultes, now Professor of Natural Sciences at Harvard University and Director of the Harvard Botanical Museum, to correct this mistaken impression.

In 1938 Schultes visited the little town of Huautla de Jimenez in the Sierra Mazateca mountains, actually obtaining specimens of the sacred mushrooms and returning with them to Harvard. A Protestant missionary and linguist, Eunice V. Pike, who had worked among the Mazatecs, also knew about them, and it was as a result of her letters, and Schultes' field study articles that the retired banker R. Gordon Wasson and his wife Valentina, embarked on their celebrated 'pilgrimage' to experience sacred mushrooms at first hand. It was Wasson who brought the issue to prominence in 1957 with an article in *Life* magazine describing, as he writes in his own words, 'the awe and reverence . . . of a shamanic mushroom agape'.[6] For those unfamiliar with Gordon Wasson's remarkable adventure, a brief summary is provided later in this chapter.

The most important of the shamanic mushrooms in Mexico is the species *Psilocybe mexicana*, which grows in wet pasture lands, although other, related types of mushrooms are also consumed.

Psilocybe mushrooms provide a state of intoxication characterised by vivid and colourful hallucinations and also unusual auditory effects. It is for the latter reason that the Mazatecs say, respectfully, that 'the mushrooms speak'.

We are extremely fortunate to have a poetic account of native mushroom practices from Henry Munn, a Westerner who has lived for many years among the Mazatecs of Oaxaca, and who married the niece of a shaman and shamaness in that society. As Munn writes in his article 'The Mushrooms of Language': 'The shamans who eat them, their function is to speak, they are the speakers who chant and sing the truth, they are the oral poets of their people, the doctors of the word, they who tell what is wrong and how to remedy it, the seers and oracles, the ones possessed by the voice.'[7]

There is also an intriguing tendency among the Mazatecs to blend native folk-traditions and mythology with Christian beliefs. According to Munn the Mazatecs say that 'Through their miraculous mountains of light and rain . . . Christ once walked – it is a transformation of the legend of Quetzalcoatl – and from where dropped his blood, the essence of his life, from there the holy mushrooms grew, the awakeners of the spirit, the food of the luminous one.'[8]

Mazatec shamans only utilise the sacred mushrooms to diagnose disease – to contact the spirits causing illness. If there is nothing wrong, there is no reason to eat them, and the mushrooms are certainly not taken recreationally.

The Aztecs were in such awe of them that they called the mushrooms *teonanacatl*, which translates as 'divine flesh'. Today they are used ritually not only by the Mazatecs, but also by the Nahua Indians of Puebla and the Tarascana of Michoacan – specifically in religious and divinatory rites. In all cases the mushrooms are taken at night in rituals accompanied by chants and invocations. Interestingly, although psychoactive mushrooms also grow in South America, they appear not to enjoy the same ritual usage in that continent, as they do in Mexico.

Morning Glory

The Morning Glory species *Rivea corymbosa* was known to the Aztecs as *ololiuhqui*, and they regarded the plant as a divinity. The seeds of this well-known flowering vine contain ergot alkaloids related to d-lysergic acid diethylamide – better known as LSD. However, the effects of Morning Glory seeds are generally of shorter duration than the LSD experience, lasting only six hours. Often associated with nausea, intake of the seeds can produce a sensation of bright lights and colour patterns, feelings of euphoria, and often profound states of peace and relaxation.

Employed these days especially by Zapotec shamans to treat sickness or to acquire powers of divination, the Morning Glory seeds are carefully prepared for ritual use. They have to be ground on a stone to produce a type of flour which is added to cold water. The beverage is then strained through cloth and consumed. If the seeds are taken whole they have no effect, passing through the body without producing hallucinations.

As with peyote, we have an early, if somewhat biased, description of *ololiuhqui* from the Spanish physician Francisco Hernandez who, in 1651, wrote of the Aztecs that 'when the priests wanted to commune with the gods and to receive a message from them, they ate this plant to induce a delirium. A thousand visions and satanic hallucinations appeared to them. In its manner of action, this plant can be compared with *Solanum maniacum* of Dioscorides. It grows in warm places in the fields.'[9]

Predictably, the ritual use of Morning Glory among the Aztecs was suppressed after the Spanish Conquest although the Aztecs continued to hide the seeds in secret locations to avoid detection and persecution. Of interest too is the Aztec mural at Teotihuacan mentioned earlier in this chapter. Thought previously to be a representation of the male rain-god Tlaloc, it is now considered to be a Mother Goddess akin to the fertility deity Xochiquetzal, and an embodiment of the Morning Glory. Gordon Wasson believes that the Aztec God of Flowers, Xochipilli, also has a link with *ololiuhqui*, being a 'patron deity of sacred hallucinogenic plants' and the 'flowery dream'.[10]

Morning Glory, or ololiuhqui

Ironically, as if to redeem their 'Satanic' associations in the minds of the Spanish conquerors, the Zapotecs of Oaxaca now refer to the Morning Glory seeds in Christian terms, calling them 'Mary's Herb' or 'The Seed of the Virgin'.

BANISTERIOPSIS

The tree-climbing forest vine known botanically as *Banisteriopsis caapi* is the pre-eminent sacred plant of South America. Its bark is brewed to make a beverage which allows direct contact with the supernatural realm, enabling shamans to contact ancestors or helper spirits and have initiatory visions.

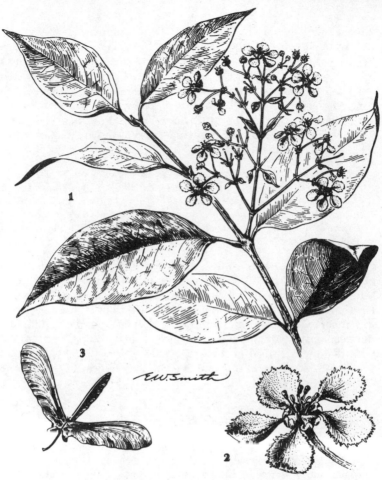

Banisteriopsis caapi – 'vine of the soul'

Among the Jivaro of Ecuador the Banisteriopsis drink is called *natema*; elsewhere it is called *caapi, yaje* or *ayahuasca* – a term which translates as 'vine of the soul'.

The hallucinogenic qualities of Banisteriopsis derive from the presence of the harmala alkaloids, harmaline and harmine – formerly known collectively as 'telepathine' because of their apparent capacity to stimulate extra-sensory perception. The drug certainly produces in many subjects – both native and Western – the sensation of the 'flight of the soul' and intensely coloured and dramatic visions. Shamans utilising *ayahuasca* report encounters with supernatural beings – the Conibo say it helps them to see demons in the air – and also, among the Jivaro, shamans have visions of giant anacondas and jaguars rolling over and over through the rain forest. The claims of enhanced telepathic faculties also appear to have some foundation. The South American anthropologist Tomas Roessner reported that members of a tribe located near the Ucayali River in Eastern Peru were genuinely surprised at the objects they 'observed' clairvoyantly in modern cities they had never visited physically:

> [The Indians] who frequently practise the use of *ayahuasca* sit at times together and, drinking it, propose that they all see something of the same subject, for example: 'Let's see cities!' It so happens that Indians have asked white men what those strange things (*aparatos*) are which run so swiftly along the street: they had seen automobiles, which, of course, they were not acquainted with.[11]

On the whole, the Banisteriopsis beverage is used to recover the souls of sick patients, to ask the spirits about the cause of bewitchment, or – in the case of sorcery – to allow the black magician to change his form into that of a bird or some other animal in order to cause harm to someone. However, the sacred drug also has the role of allowing the shaman to participate in his own cosmology, to 'become one with the mythic world of the Creation'. Gerardo Reichel-Dolmatoff provides these details of shamanic visions experienced by the Tukano Indians of Colombia:

> According to the Tukano, after a stage of undefined luminosity of moving forms and colours, the vision begins to clear up and significant details present themselves. The Milky Way appears and the distant fertilising reflection of the Sun. The first woman surges forth from the waters of the river, and first pair of ancestors is formed. The supernatural Master of the Animals of the jungle and waters is perceived, as are the gigantic prototypes of the game animals, and the origins of plants – indeed, the origins of life itself. The origins of Evil also manifest themselves, jaguars and serpents, the representatives of illness, and the spirits of the jungle that lie in ambush for the solitary hunter. At the same time their voices are heard, the music of the mythic epoch is perceived, and the ancestors are seen, dancing at the dawn of Creation. The origin of the ornaments used in dances, the feather crowns, necklace, armlets, and musical instruments, are all seen. The division into phratries is witnessed, and the *yurupari* flutes promulgate the laws of exogamy. Beyond these visions new 'doors' are opening, and through the apertures glimmer yet other dimensions, which are even more profound .. For the Indian the hallucinatory experience

is essentially a sexual one. To make it sublime, to pass from the erotic, the sensual, to a mystical union with the mythic era, the intra-uterine stage, is the ultimate goal, attained by a mere handful, but coveted by all. We find the most cogent expression of this objective in the words of an Indian educated by missionaries, who said: 'To take *yaje* is a spiritual coitus; it is the spiritual communion which the priests speak of.'[12]

On a more basic level, Banisteriopsis is considered simply as a powerful medicine, as a means of healing, and a way of acquiring special knowledge. The Cashinahua regard the visions they experience as portents of things to come and view the sacrament as 'a fearsome thing' – something regarded with awe and very much respected. The Jivaro, meanwhile, consider that their helper spirits, *tsentsak*, can only be seen in *natema*-induced visions and since disease is caused primarily by witchcraft, the sacred drug allows access to the sources of the trouble. Some *tsentsak* spirits also provide a type of psychic shield against magical attack.

TOBACCO

Strictly speaking, tobacco is an intoxicant rather than a hallucinogen, although it is used shamanically in some parts of South America.

The Campa Indians of the Eastern Peruvian rain forest combine tobacco and *ayahuasca* as a shamanic sacrament but regard the tobacco in itself as a source of power. Used in nocturnal rituals, the combination of tobacco and Banisteriopsis produces an altered state of consciousness in which the shaman's voice takes on a eerie quality. As he begins to sing, the shaman's soul may go to some distant place, but the words themselves are those of the spirits – the trance allowing direct communication. 'When the shaman sings he is only repeating what he hears the spirits sing,' writes Gerald Weiss; 'he is merely singing along with them. At no time is he possessed by a spirit, since Campa culture does not include a belief in spirit possession.'[13]

The following shaman-song indicates that tobacco is revered in its own right:

> Tobacco, tobacco, pure tobacco,
> It comes from River's Beginning
> *Kaokiti*, the hawk, brings it to you
> Its flowers are flying, tobacco
> It comes to your [or our] aid, tobacco
> Tobacco, tobacco, pure tobacco
> *Kaokiti*, the hawk, is its owner

The Warao Indian shamans of Venezuela, meanwhile, undertake periods of fasting and then smoke large cigars made of strong, native tobacco to induce a state of narcotic trance. The Warao believe that the earth is surrounded by water and that both the earth and ocean in turn are covered by a celestial vault. At the cardinal and inter-cardinal points, the vault rests on a series of mountains, and Supreme Spirits (*Kanobos*) dwell in these mountains at the edge of the world.

The priest-shaman, or *wishiratu*, is able to visit these spirits during tobacco-induced trance journeys, even though the journeys are themselves fraught with such an assortment of obstacles and perils that one would hardly think the journeys worthwhile! To begin with, the shaman journeys towards the *manaca* palm – the shamanic tree of all *wishiratus* – and then travels to a series of water-holes where he can drink and purify himself. He then has to clear an abyss where jaguars, alligators, sharks and spear-bearing demons threaten to destroy him. He is also likely to encounter sexually provocative women, whom he must resist, and also a giant hawk with a savage beak and flapping wings. These the shaman must pass by without temptation or fear – only then is he nearing his goal:

> Finally the candidate shaman has to pass through a hole in an enormous tree trunk with rapidly opening and closing doors. He hears the voice of his guide and companion from the other side of the trunk, for this spirit has already cleared the dangerous passage and now encourages the fearful novice to follow his example. The candidate jumps through the clashing doors and looks around inside the hollow tree. There he beholds a huge serpent with four colourful horns and a fiery-red luminous ball on the tip of her protruding tongue. This serpent has a servant with reptilean body and human head whom the candidate sees carrying away the bones of novices who failed to clear the clashing doors.
>
> The novice hurries outside and finds himself at the end of the cosmos. His patron *Kanobo's* mountain rises before him. Here he will be given a small house of his own, where he may sojourn in his future trances to consult with the *Kanobo* and where eventually he will come to live forever upon successful completion of his shaman's life on earth.[14]

SAN PEDRO CACTUS

Dating back at least three thousand years as a ritual sacrament, San Pedro cactus (*Trichocereus pachanoi*) is one of the most ancient magical plants of South America. The Spanish noticed shamans in

Peru drinking a beverage made from its sap and, essentially, this process still continues. Today it is cut into slices, boiled for around seven hours in water, and then consumed to bring on the visions. In Peru it is known simply as San Pedro, in Bolivia, Achuma. Purchased by shamans at the markets, the cactus contains mescaline and initially produces drowsiness and a state of dreamy lethargy. However, this is followed by a remarkable lucidity of mental faculties. Finally, one may experience 'a telepathic sense of transmitting oneself across time and matter'.

Shamans in Peru and Bolivia utilise the cactus to contact spirits, to treat illness, to counteract the dangers of witchcraft, and for purposes of divination.

EDUARDO CALDERÓN – PERUVIAN HEALER

We owe an undoubted debt to anthropologist Douglas Sharon for bringing to light the shamanism of Eduardo Calderón – a Peruvian shaman whose cosmology includes Christian as well as native Indian elements, and who utilises San Pedro cactus in his workings. Sharon first met Eduardo Calderón in 1965 and undertook an apprenticeship with him in 1970. As a result we now have not only Sharon's anthropological accounts of Calderón's magical universe but the unique documentary film *Eduardo the Healer*, completed in 1978.

Calderón was born in Trujillo in 1930 and grew up in a Spanish-speaking Roman Catholic family. Initially, he hoped to study religion or medicine. Later he took a course in Fine Arts in Lima, funded by money which he earned as a bricklayer, and in subsequent years worked variously as a tuna fisherman and ceramist, producing replicas of ancient pottery vessels for tourists. However, both his grandfathers were *curanderos* from the Peruvian highlands, and not surprisingly Eduardo discovered he had inner yearnings in this direction as well. According to Sharon, Eduardo had special dreams urging him to 'prepare himself', and when he was 22 he was cured of an ailment by a folk-healer – orthodox medicine on this occasion having proved of no avail.

Another influence on Eduardo's spiritual development was the uncle of his second wife: this man was a *curandero* also, and used both San Pedro and a *mesa* – an altar containing various magical 'power objects'. At the age of 24, Eduardo began an apprenticeship with the uncle and on one occasion was called in to treat a sick cousin using the same shamanic approach that he had been taught. After this he was able to establish himself as a *curandero* in his own right.

San Pedro cactus is grown mainly in the region around Huancabamba, close to the border between Peru and Ecuador, and many shamans make pilgrimages there to obtain their sacraments. Others send friends on their behalf. Thinner cacti are preferred, and they are sliced like bread and boiled in water for several hours. Usually nothing else is added, although some shamans mix San Pedro with datura. Calderón believed that the cactus, and magical herbs in general, had great shamanic value: 'The herbs have their spirits – because they speak [and] direct the activities in the realm of curanderismo during the nocturnal session . . . [the spirits] can advise or warn him.'[15]

However, he also believed that the healer could emit a power to the plants, infusing them with the intellectual and spiritual qualities of humankind. The San Pedro and other magical plants 'provide a medium by which [the healer's] contact with the earth is renewed in a reciprocal flow of energy'.

One of the most intriguing facets of Eduardo's healing sessions was his mesa. This magical altar had two 'fields', representing zones of good and evil, and also a type of middle ground – a neutral zone where the opposing forces were held in balance. The polarities of the mesa were crucial to Eduardo's· healing power because associated with each zone were artefacts of different symbolic value. The smaller left zone associated with Satan had three demonic staffs, for example, whereas the right-hand zone, ruled by Christ, had artefacts representative of positive magic – images of saints, holy water, various perfumes and cans of San Pedro infusion. Christ also had eight staffs allocated to him, including the sword of St Paul and the sword of St James the Elder. Then, in the middle field, were objects of magical neutrality – a glass jar containing magical herbs, a crystal mirror, and a statue of St Cyprian, ruler of that particular zone.

According to Douglas Sharon the artefacts on the mesa provided 'a focal point of a particular force. Collectively, they are a projection of [Eduardo's] own inner spiritual power, which becomes activated whenever the mesa is manipulated in conjunction with the drinking of the hallucinogenic San Pedro infusion.'[16]

The healing session begins at night. Eduardo undertakes various ceremonial activities from 10 a.m. until midnight and the diagnosis, aided by the visionary effects of San Pedro, can last until 4 a.m. Any night of the week is suitable for a healing ceremony except Monday, when dead souls from purgatory are likely to be roaming about.

Following the ceremonial chants and invocations, which last until midnight, all present partake of San Pedro. For Eduardo the curandero this infusion 'activates' the artefacts on the mesa, enabling him to 'see' the cause of witchcraft or bad luck afflicting his client. Once such a cause of evil has been perceived in this magical way, it can then be ritually exorcised.

Eduardo was quite explicit in explaining to Douglas Sharon how the healing power was initially invoked:

> I salute the ancients, the powerful ones, men who have lived in antiquity . . . for their intellectual force, their power, their magnificence, and the saints for their . . . intellect, their personality . . . their great power as philosophers, writers, poets . . . [so] that they will help me intellectually in search of these inconveniences [i.e. the causes of the patient's problems] in order to discover a solution. I always invoke the ancients, brujos, curanderos who have died [and] who are alive, calling their spirits, their personalities. They attend and deliver ideas that can bring one out of trance, out of the wrong path that he may be following. Therefore I [also] call on St Augustine, Moses, Solomon, St Cyprian, St Paul, for advice, for help in moments of doubt.[17]

However, educated as he was, and able to communicate with Sharon in a terminology he could understand, Eduardo also explained that San Pedro enabled him to 'visualise' and open up a 'sixth sense' – thus allowing him to have an intimate perception of his client's psyche:

> The subconscious is a superior part [of man] . . . a kind of bag where the individual has stored all his memories . . . all his valuations. One must try . . . to make the individual 'jump out' of his conscious mind. That is the principal task of curanderismo. By means of the magical plants and the chants and the search for the roots of the problem, the subconscious of the individual is opened like a flower.[18]

Sharon also sums up the healing process very succinctly. 'What emerges', he writes, 'is that the hallucinogenic San Pedro cactus is experienced as the catalyst that enables the curandero to transcend the limitations placed on ordinary mortals; to activate all his senses; project his spirit or soul; ascend and descend into the supernatural realms; identify and do battle with the sources of illness . . . "to see".'[19]

GORDON WASSON AND THE SACRED MUSHROOMS

For R. Gordon Wasson the shamanic pilgrimage came late in life. Born in 1898, Wasson had had a career in newspapers and banking, rising to the position of vice-president with J. P. Morgan & Co. in New York. Wasson and his Russian-born wife Valentina had read the Mexican field reports of Richard Evans Schultes and had communicated with Eunice V. Pike about the secret mushroom ceremonies of the Mazatec Indians. So it was, that on three occasions between 1953 and 1955 they went to Mexico 'as Pilgrims seeking the Grail' – to use their own phrase – to see if they could uncover firsthand evidence of the use of sacred mushrooms.

The Wassons had as a guide Austrian Robert Weitlaner, who had studied the Mazatecs for many years and who accompanied them on their first mule-ride to the Sierra Mazateca. He would also travel with them on subsequent trips.

In June 1955 the Wassons arrived in the town of Huautla, together with their daughter Masha, and Allan Richardson – a friend and photographer. After pondering for some time how he would actually contact the shamans – who presumably worked in secret and shunned strangers – Wasson approached a town official, Cayetano Garcia, to ask if he knew anyone who could help him learn the secrets of the sacred mushrooms, or *ntixitjo* – as they were known to the Mazatecs. Fortunately, Garcia was receptive and invited Wasson to come to his home during the siesta, late in the afternoon.

When Wasson and Allan Richardson arrived they were subsequently taken to a place in a nearby gully where the sacred mushrooms were growing on a bed of refuse from a cane-mill. They gathered some mushrooms in a box and returned to Garcia's house.

Garcia then directed Wasson, with his brother Emilio acting as interpreter, to seek out a renowned shamaness, Maria Sabina, to provide help that night. Fortunately she agreed to participate, and said she would come to Cayetano's after dark.

At the time, Maria Sabina was a woman in her fifties, and was highly regarded by the Mazatec community as *una Senora sin mancha* – a lady without blemish. This first night was to be one of several all-night vigils, or *veladas*, that she, Gordon Wasson, Allan Richardson and other local residents, would undertake together.

That night, after Maria Sabina had arrived, they all ate the sacred mushrooms together. Since the Mazatecs regard the mushrooms with reverence, they were eaten in respectful silence near a small altar table. Cayetano's father, don Emilio, intended to consult the sacred mushrooms about his left forearm, which was infected, but for Wasson it would be a much more all-encompassing initiatory experience. He did not especially enjoy the acrid taste of the mushrooms, but shortly before midnight it was apparent that the effects were coming on. Eventually, as Wasson writes, they took 'full and sweeping possession' of him:

> There is no better way to describe the sensation than to say that it was as though my very soul had been scooped out of my body and translated to a point floating in space, leaving behind the husk of clay, my body. Our bodies lay there while our souls soared . . .
>
> At first we saw geometric patterns, angular not circular, in richest colours, such as might adorn textiles or carpets. Then the patterns grew into architectural structures, with colonnades and architraves, patios of regal splendour, the stone-work all in brilliant colours, gold and onyx and ebony, all most harmoniously and ingeniously contrived, in richest magnificence extending beyond the reach of sight. For some reason these architectural visions seemed oriental, though at every stage I pointed out to myself that they could not be identified with any specific oriental country. They were neither Japanese nor Chinese nor Indian nor Moslem. They seemed to belong rather to the imaginary architecture described by the visionaries of the Bible. In the aesthetics of this discovered world Attic simplicity had no place: everything was resplendently rich.
>
> At one point in the faint moonlight the bouquet on the table assumed the dimensions and shape of an imperial conveyance, a triumphal car, drawn by zoological creatures conceivable only in an imaginary mythology, bearing a woman clothed in regal splendour. With our eyes wide open, the visions came in endless succession, each growing out of the preceding one. We had the sensation that the walls of our humble house had vanished, that our untrammelled souls were floating in the empyrean, stroked by divine breezes, possessed of a divine mobility that would transport us anywhere on the wings of a thought. Now it was clear why don Aurelio in 1953 and others too had told us that the mushrooms *le llevan ahi donde Dios esta* – would take you there where God is. Only when by an act of conscious effort I touched the wall of Cayetano's house would I be brought back to the confines of the room where we all were.[20]

During each *velada* – Wasson attended two during his 1955 visit to Huautla – Maria Sabina would take thirteen pairs of mushrooms while the visiting participants took five or six pairs each. Maria Sabina explained to Gordon Wasson that the purpose of a *velada* was to enable the patient to consult with the shaman about something that was worrying them – an illness, theft, a loss of some kind, or the causes of an accident. During the *velada* the mushrooms would then speak through the voice of the shaman – the mushrooms literally 'uttering the word'. The pronouncements would then be conveyed to the patient.

To achieve this divinely inspired communication, Maria Sabina – and also her daughter, who took a similar number of mushrooms, and acted as an assistant – would initially hum and chant, both in Mazatec and Spanish. They would then invoke the spirits of the sacred mushroom. Maria has herself explained the effect of the sacred inebriation: 'I see the Word fall, come down from above, as though they were little luminous objects falling from heaven. The Word falls on the Holy Table, on my body: with my hand I catch them, Word by Word.'[21]

Maria Sabina's emphasis on 'the Word' is also confirmed by Henry Munn who, as we have seen, similarly refers to 'the mushrooms of language' among the Mazatecs. But it is important to remember that it is a sacred language we are talking about here. It is the God who is speaking. The mushrooms are an embodiment of the divine Logos. Through the sacred mushroom, the Word has become flesh.

6 · THE SHAMANS SPEAK

There have been many shamans through history, each with a special way of perceiving the world. Many of these we can know only through myth, legend or song, but some – like Eduardo Calderón and Maria Sabina – have left their mark on cultural history as individuals, and their stories have been recorded for others to appreciate.

In this chapter are further profiles of notable shamans who have made a unique contribution to the visionary perspective. Each, in his or her own way, has experienced a special encounter with the Spirit which had led to a feeling of renewal – a revitalising of both the inner and outer worlds.

BLACK ELK

Black Elk was an Oglala Sioux holy man – a *wichasha wakon* – who had been part of the Messianic movement that ended with the massacre at Wounded Knee in 1890. Born in 1863 at Little Powder River, he was also the second cousin of Crazy Horse, the famous chieftain who had led the Sioux in the Indian Wars.

When his biographer, John G. Neihardt, met him in August 1930, Black Elk was nearly blind, but he was willing to recount in detail the remarkable visionary episodes which had transformed his life. Neihardt was a white man, but fortunately he was welcomed as an adopted member of the Oglala Sioux and accepted as an intermediary to help Black Elk communicate his visions to a broader audience. Black Elk's son, Ben, acted as a translator and Neihardt helped shape the various incidents and memories into a coherent chronological sequence. In this way the volume now known as *Black Elk Speaks* gradually took form. It was first published in 1932 and has been translated into several languages. Black Elk died in August 1950.

For Black Elk the call to shamanism came early in life. When he was 5 he had a spontaneous shamanic experience and as he said himself: 'This was not a dream, it happened.' As he looked up at the sky, two human figures seemed to descend from the clouds: 'they sang a sacred song and the thunder was like drumming . . . The song and the drumming went like this:

'Behold, a sacred voice is calling you;
All over the sky a sacred voice is calling.'

'I sat there gazing at them,' Black Elk told Neihardt,' and they were coming from the place where the giant lives [north]. But when they were very close to me, they wheeled about toward where the sun goes down, and suddenly they were geese. Then they were gone, and the rain came with a big wind and a roaring. I did not tell this vision to anyone. I liked to think about it, but I was afraid to tell it.'[1]

Then, when he was 9, further revelations occurred. Black Elk's family had camped near a creek which ran into the Little Big Horn River and he was resting in his tepee. Unexpectedly Black Elk heard a voice quite distinctly: 'It is time, now they are calling you.' He came out of his tepee – 'it was like waking from a dream' – and looked around but there was no one there, and no voice. He noticed, however, that his legs were hurting him.

The following morning when he was riding with some other boys Black Elk stopped by a creek and when he got off his horse his legs crumpled beneath him. His friends helped him back onto his horse but he became quite sick and seemed badly swollen all over.

Next day, as he lay in his tepee, he could see through the opening and once again two men appeared to come down through the clouds – they were the same figures he had seen four years earlier. 'Each now carried a long spear, and from the points of these a jagged lightning flashed. They came down to the ground this time and stood a little way off and looked at me and said: "Hurry! Come! Your Grandfathers are calling you!"[2]

Black Elk was clearly experiencing a sense of dissociation for as he now 'rose' his legs did not hurt and he felt 'very light'. He now began what was really a classical shamanic journey:

> I went outside the tepee, and yonder where the men with flaming spears were going, a little cloud was coming very fast. It came and stopped and took me and turned back to where it came from, flying fast. And when I looked down I could see my mother and my father yonder, and I felt sorry to be leaving them.
>
> Then there was nothing but the air and the swiftness of the little cloud that bore me and those two men still leading up to where white clouds were piled like mountains on a wide blue plain, and in them the thunder beings lived and leaped and flashed.
>
> Now suddenly there was nothing but a world of cloud, and we three were there alone in the middle of a great white plain with snowy hills and mountains staring at us; and it was very still; but there were whispers.[3]

Black Elk now had a dramatic and very beautiful vision of twelve majestic horses appearing in the west with lightning flashing in their manes and thunder roaring from their nostrils. This was followed by three further visions of similar groups of horses – each of different colours in turn, and appearing from different directions – and the heavens seemed to trumpet with the stamping of their hooves. After dancing through the sky the horses then transformed 'into animals of every kind', fled to the four quarters of the world, and disappeared.

Now, rising before him, Black Elk saw within the clouds a formation that became a tepee, and also a rainbow which became its open door. Through the door he could see six old men sitting in a row:

> The two men with the spears now stood beside me, one on either hand, and the horses took their places in their quarters, looking inward, four by four. And the oldest of the Grandfathers spoke with a kind voice and said: 'Come right in and do not fear.' As he spoke, all the horses of the four quarters neighed to cheer me. So I went in and stood before the six, and they looked older than men can ever be – old like hills, like stars.
>
> The oldest spoke again: 'Your Grandfathers all over the world are having a council, and they have called you here to teach you.'[4]

destroy), a herb (for healing), a peace-pipe with a seemingly live eagle on its stem, and a bright red stick which sprouted like a Tree of Life.

A tragedy would befall the American Indians . . . (collage by Wilfried Satty)

Overcome by awe, Black Elk now realised that the 'Grandfathers' were no ordinary ancestors – they were in fact the Powers of the World. They now, in turn, bestowed upon him a water-filled wooden cup (representing the powers of life), a bow (with the power to

btm 65

Black Elk now embarked upon a series of mythic encounters through the heavens, witnessing dramatic scenes of violence and renewal, and passing through four specific 'ascents', apparently representing the future of the American Indians on the planet.

The first ascent, and the most idyllic sequence, featured a holy tree (the characteristic World Tree of the shaman) and the land all about was green and luxuriant. However, each subsequent ascent revealed phases of the ensuing tragedy that would befall the American Indians. During the second ascent the people transformed into animals of the hunt and grew restless and afraid. Leaves began to fall from the holy tree. Then, in the third ascent, the animals seemed to run amok and, as Black Elk recounted, 'all over the universe I could hear the winds at war like wild beasts fighting.' By now the holy tree seemed to be dying and the birds that formerly dwelt in its branches had departed.

In the fourth ascent there were further pitiful scenes portraying the tragic demise of the American Indians. The tribesfolk had become human again, rather than animal, but they were thin and starving, and the holy tree had now disappeared. 'It was dark and terrible about me, for all the winds of the world were fighting. It was like rapid gun-fire and like whirling smoke, and like women and children wailing and like horses screaming all over the world.'

However, at this crucial point in the visions a song of power was given to Black Elk and, as he relates, 'I sang it there in the midst of that terrible place . . .

A good nation I will make live.
This the nation above has said.
They have given me the power to make over.'[5]

Black Elk now found himself riding upon a horse which had been transformed from a lean and miserable specimen into a shining black stallion – all this by the 'herb of power'. After addressing the four quarters on his steed, four virgin women appeared – 'more beautiful than women of the earth can be' – one holding the wooden cup of water, one a white wing, one a peace-pipe and one 'the hoop of the Nation'. The universe now fell silent as the black stallion sang a song of power which 'was so beautiful that nothing anywhere could keep from dancing'. As Black Elk recalled:

The virgins danced, and all the circled horses. The leaves on the trees, the grasses on the hills and in the valleys, the waters in the creeks and in the rivers and the lakes, the four-legged and two-legged and the wings of the air – all danced together to the music of the stallion's song.

And when I looked down upon my people yonder, the cloud passed over, blessing them with friendly rain, and stood in the east with a flaming rainbow over it.[6]

Black Elk was now transported, like an archetypal shaman, to the centre of the world:

> I was standing on the highest mountain of them all, and round about beneath me was the whole hoop of the world. And while I stood there I saw more than I can tell and I understood more than I saw; for I was seeing in a sacred manner the shapes of all things in the spirit, and the shape of all shapes as they must live together like one being. And I saw that the sacred hoop of my people was one of many hoops that made one circle, wide as daylight and as starlight, and in the centre grew one mighty flowering tree to shelter all the children of one mother and one father. And I saw that it was holy.[7]

As Black Elk returned to the tepee of the six Grandfathers there was much rejoicing. Black Elk was told triumphantly that he must now return to his people. The oldest Grandfather began to sing a sacred song, and Black Elk became aware that he was returning to his village tepee:

> I saw my own tepee, and inside I saw my mother and my father, bending over a sick boy that was myself. And as I entered the tepee, someone was saying: 'The boy is coming to; you had better give him some water.'
> Then I was sitting up; and I was sad because my mother and my father didn't seem to know I had been so far away.[8]

Black Elk initially kept his vision a secret but keeping it stored up inside him made him listless and 'crazy'. Then, when he was 16, he began to experience a renewed inner calling. It seemed that he would have to manifest his vision in some way. He heard the song of the daybreak star:

> 'In a sacred manner you shall walk,
> Your nation shall behold you!'

A medicine-man named Black Road had been summoned to treat Black Elk's continuing 'malaise' and when Black Elk told him what had happened, the medicine-man said he would have to perform his vision for everyone to see. The mythic encounter would have to be grounded.

A short time after his seventeenth birthday, preparations for Black Elk's 'horse dance' got underway. Black Road and another Indian, Bear Sings, organised a sacred tepee and painted on it different motifs from Black Elk's visionary journeys – the cup, the geese, the pipe, the flowering stick and so on. Black Elk had to undergo a purificatory sweat-bath and also teach Black Road and Bear Sings the songs which he had been given in his visions. In due course other members of the tribe also took the roles of the Grandfathers, the maidens, and the warriors with their horses. Each in turn then performed ceremonially the major events of Black Elk's vision – the dances, the parading of horses, the singing of sacred songs.

Then, at one point, a remarkable thing happened. All of the horses in the village seemed to neigh in unison and, as Black Elk looked up toward the heavens, once again he beheld his vision. It was as if the mythic world and the physical world had become one:

> Suddenly, as I sat there looking at the cloud, I saw my vision yonder once again – the tepee built of cloud and sewed with lightning, the flaming rainbow door and, underneath, the Six Grandfathers sitting, and all the horses thronging in their quarters; and also there was I myself upon my bay before the tepee. I looked about me and could see that what we then were doing was like a shadow cast upon the earth from yonder vision in the heavens, so bright it was and clear. I knew the real was yonder and the darkened dream of it was here.[9]

Here was dramatic confirmation of Black Elk's ceremonial undertaking to share his visions with his people. Clearly the Grandfathers had observed the ritual re-enactment and were well pleased . . . The peace-pipe was now passed around and a sense of renewal seemed to pervade the community:

> After the horse dance was over, it seemed that I was above the ground and did not touch it when I walked. I felt very happy, for I could see that my people were all happier. Many crowded around me and said that they or their relatives who had been feeling sick were well again, and these gave me many gifts. Even the horses seemed to be healthier and happier after the dance.[10]

LUISAH TEISH

Now in her early forties, Luisah Teish was born in New Orleans of mixed African, Haitian, Choctaw and French ancestry and brings to her spiritual perspective a diverse range of influences. Raised in New Orleans, nominally a Roman Catholic but increasingly as a practitioner of Voudou, she is now also a priestess of the Nigerian Yoruba religion *Lucumi*. But this is not all. Today she is a dancer, a choreographer, a singer, a shaman, a healer, and a writer – her

Cinetel Productions

Luisah Teish

book *Jambalaya: The Natural Woman's Book of Personal Charms and Practical Rituals* was published in San Francisco in 1985.

Teish (pronounced 'Teesh') – as she likes to be called – describes herself as originally 'Louisiana Catholic': a polite expression for one who follows Voudou with a thin veneer of Christianity over the top.

It wasn't a case of deliberately pursuing magic, Teish told me when I first met her in California in 1984, so much as waiting for it to happen. The elders would perform secret rites around her as she was growing up and watch for omens, or for significant traits to emerge in her personality. Teish's mother wanted her to be a nurse or a teacher, and would ignore her questions about 'women's mysteries'. Nevertheless, Teish found she had an innate capacity for prophetic dreams and would frequently sleepwalk. She learnt magical cures by fossicking around for bits of information, and also gleaned insights into occult ways of reading weather patterns and interpreting animal behaviour. Teish explained that there is a paranoid element among Voudou practitioners in the deep south because practising traditional African religion on the slave plantations was punishable by death. Voudou instead became incorporated into domestic routine that wouldn't be noticed by the slave owners.

Teish recounts a fascinating event from her youth:

> When I was a little girl my mother used to send me to the Catholic church and she would tell me, 'Go and ask Father Fitzpatrick for a little holy water.' You know, she'd send me with a jar and I'd go get the holy water from the church, and she'd put it in a bucket with sugar, urine and a little perfume. Then she'd get a picture of one of the saints and mop the floor, and the whole time she was mopping the floor she was telling the saint what she wanted to have happening in her house – magically that is. That's what I call being 'Louisiana Catholic', where you're Catholic on the surface but there's a lot more going on underneath.[11]

Teish says that her 'entire childhood was filled with visions and intuitions and the whispered guidance of a spirit guide whom I call "She Who Whispers"'. Psychic forces raged inside her and did not begin to manifest fully until her early twenties when she decided to confront her mother about her magical practices by tricking her into becoming a confidante. Teish announced that she was going to make a magical charm with graveyard dust. Her mother clearly recognised that Teish was ready for the secrets, and confided to her daughter that she was a medium and a member of an 'altar circle'. They have been 'good buddies' over since.

Teish also says that learning dance with Katherine Dunham's group in the late 1960s helped her to free her psychic energies. Dunham had worked as an anthropologist, preserving the native dance traditions of Africa and Haiti, and Teish found that by working with her and performing these dances she was able to tap the primal impulses of her ancestral heritage. During one particular dance – *Damballah* – she had an out-of-the body experience.

Some time after this, Teish joined the Fahami Temple of the Egyptian sun-god Amun-Ra and underwent a lengthy initiation which helped her appreciate her African spiritual roots even more. Her specific orientation is now the *Lucumi* tradition of West Africa.

For Luisah Teish the spiritual universe offers contact with the consciousness of the ancestors – called Eguns – and the consciousness of Nature – called Orishas. Eguns have lived before on the planet but Orishas are elemental energies in Nature like the river, wind, fire and ocean. Each Orisha has its own power, but some take a role of special prominence. Yemaya, for example, is the Mother of the Earth Spirits, a personification of the ocean, dreams, healing and cleansing. Teish says her mystery is unfathomable – 'Nobody knows what's at the bottom of the ocean' – but at the same time she feels a very close and respectful relationship with her: 'She is incredibly beautiful, incredibly powerful and wise.' Then there is the sky-god Obatala, representing the clouds, creativity, and the wisdom that comes with old age. He, too, is a friend. In fact, Teish says of the Orishas that 'the entire pantheon is so human that you don't feel like you are bowing to a superior. You feel like you have a relative or a friend with *extra* human powers who can help you.'

However, Teish's special bond is with Oshun, the Nigerian counterpart of the Roman goddess Venus, who is known also as 'Mother of the Spirit'. As Teish told writer Mimi Albert:

> I am a child of Oshun ... I will sing the praise of Oshun all day long. Oshun is a river goddess, the goddess of the sweet waters. She is also the goddess of love. ... Oshun's colour is the bright yellow of illumination and wealth; her favourite foods are very sweet, very seedy, very leafy. Pumpkin, with all the seeds inside and its bright orange colour, is one of her foods; she also loves pastries and sweets and fruits of all kinds. She's the goddess of cooking, among other things, so we associate a well-laid table, with flowers, candles and gourmet dishes, with Oshun.[12]

According to Teish, the Goddess lies asleep in the crown chakra – the psychic energy centre in the head. When a person is ritually initiated, the magical herbs and songs arouse the spirit, and the devotee is possessed by Goddess. For her, magical dance in a Goddess ceremony has a very powerful effect. As she explains, it induces a state of trance and also the feeling of being out of the body:

> Suddenly I find I'm dancing off-rhythm, and an ancestor or a spirit is there. You are bombarded by music, and not really in control of your body. It seems that the drummer's hands are your feet and then at some point there is a great silence. You find you are now on the wall, on the ceiling – over there somewhere – watching your body performing ...
>
> It's very invigorating. The body seems to be able to do things in trance that you cannot do when you're fully conscious. Bursts of energy come in and take over![13]

Teish's magic is mostly benevolent and people come to her mostly for spiritual advice, or for wealth and love charms. She claims to be able to reverse black magic, but rarely inflicts harmful magic on others. 'Before doing that,' she says with a grin, 'I'd have to check with the gods first!'

However, Teish believes her main role is now to help others tune into a universal religious awareness that goes beyond sectarian differences and recognises spirituality as a global phenomenon. She maintains that the true meaning of the word *voudou* is 'life-force' and says that her shamanic perspective focuses on helping to build an environmental understanding that acknowledges the sanctity of Nature. 'I do have a basic faith in Nature's tendency to survive . . .' she said recently, reflecting on the near tragedy of Chernobyl. 'The closer we get to the possibility of total destruction, the more Nature will cause a change in basic consciousness to come about.'[14]

BROOKE MEDICINE EAGLE

Brooke Medicine Eagle provides an interesting example of how shamanism can link the old and the new – her lineage and ancestry point back towards the traditional ways of the American Indians but she has also been educated at a Western university and has utilised various holistic health therapies in formulating her world-view. She sees herself as, and indeed she is, a bridge between different cultures.

Brooke Medicine Eagle is of Sioux and Nez Perce extraction although she was raised on the Crow Reservation in Montana. The great-great-grandniece of Nez Perce holy man, Grandfather Joseph, Brooke Medicine Eagle was brought up in very modest circumstances and in comparative isolation. Together with her parents and brother, she lived ten miles from the closest reservation village and nearly sixty miles over dirt roads from any major town. She says that the initial desire to be a healer-shaman came substantially from within her own experience.

On the other hand, Brooke Medicine Eagle's links with Western culture came mostly through her education. She won a scholarship to the University of Denver, graduated with a Bachelor's degree in psychology and mathematics and then earned a Master's in psychology, specialising in counselling. Since then she has also been strongly influenced by the bodywork approach of Moshe Feldenkrais and also by the system of neuro-linguistic programming formulated by Dr John Grinder and Richard Bandler. The way these have helped her shamanic perspective is quite fascinating.

Moshe Feldenkrais was a Russian-born Israeli educator who emphasised the importance of awareness in human functioning. Awareness, he believed, could not be taught verbally but had to be experienced. With this in mind he developed a system of body movements aimed at undoing the emotional and cultural programming inflicted on people from childhood and replacing it with new ways of expressing natural impulses. Those working with the Feldenkrais method would often speak of feeling exhilarated and more alive in their movements.

For Brooke Medicine Eagle this concept is also part of shamanism. She emphasises the importance of expanding beyond artificial boundaries and limitations of movement and has compared the experience of literally being 'fenced in' by Western methods of defining land-areas with the sheer joy of riding for twenty or thirty miles on horseback in her home reservation in Montana. For her, the Western way of thinking tends often to be restrictive, inhibiting. 'Most of us think of life as a path,' she says, 'the best being the straight and narrow, where we can plod along without change. I think life is more like flying a glider.'[15]

Following on from this, one of the features of the group-work she now undertakes is an exercise in overcoming fear and literally 'flying' into the unknown. Brooke Medicine Eagle has on her ranch what she calls her 'high-challenge ropes course' which consists of a system of ropes, wires and balancing logs, many of them high above the ground. One particular platform is 55 feet high and it is connected to a zip-line which extends downward for some 500 feet. While there are in-built safety precautions, participants who mount the platform and leap off along the zip-line have to overcome their intense fears – and also learn a new sense of poise and balance prior to leaping forth. It is a challenging but also exhilarating experience, and according to Brooke Medicine Eagle its lessons are intrinsic to shamanic philosophy: 'The challenge is to play on the edge – the edge of the unformed. Part of the shaman's way is that exquisite balance – between light and dark, in and out, left and right, formless and formed.'[16]

Allied to her interest in Feldenkrais's system of Awareness Through Movement is her study of neuro-linguistic programming, or NLP. The term derives from the Greek word *neuron*, 'nerve', and the Latin, *lingua*, 'language', and indicates that there is a sensory factor in all forms of behaviour which in turn affects the structure and sequence of different forms of communication. The programming factor relates to habitual thought and behaviour patterns which affect certain outcomes.

Many forms of behaviour do not produce satisfactory outcomes and may lead to psychosomatic disease, aberrant perceptions of life, or states of being well below optimal levels of functioning. The NLP therapist observes the client's behavioural and linguistic patterns, and endeavours to guide the person beyond personal limitations to new levels of awareness and personal effectiveness.

For Brooke Medicine Eagle, NLP has highlighted the way that Western culture leads so often to programming behaviour and perpetuating habits – as she says, 'putting a form on things'. The trouble with this is that the more we reside in our habitual behaviour patterns the less able we are to be open to acquiring new knowledge. This, too, is where shamanism can be beneficial. 'My work', she says, 'is about finding ways to help us move as shamans have: to challenge the darkness; to awaken ourselves by breaking through daily habitual form into Spirit.' Speaking again in the metaphorical language she is fond of she says we should all learn new ways of 'changing with the breeze, moving like water. If we hold tight to a form – any form – I think we lose it.'[17]

These aspects of her world-view notwithstanding, Brooke Medicine Eagle has also come through a traditional Native American initiatory process. Her actual name, which can also be written as Little-Sister-of-the-Eagle, came to her through dreams and visions, and more recently she has also been given a new spiritual name, Chalise, by her inner guides. This name means 'a chalice overflowing with light'. 'My challenge', she says, 'is to truly become a chalice to receive and channel light.' She feels that one of her special spiritual tasks is to create 'a pillar of light that holds up the sky', and indeed, light is central to her vision of shamanism. 'As we lighten up in all ways, we become less dense, more filled with Spirit. Earth and physical bodies are the densest experience our eternal spirit can have; our challenge is to fill and balance it with the lightness of Spirit.'[18]

Brooke Medicine Eagle took her shamanic vision quest with an 85-year-old-Northern Cheyenne shamaness called The Woman Who Knows. Together with a younger medicine-woman they journeyed to a place called Bear Butte, near the Black Hills of South Dakota. This region had been used for hundreds of years by the Sioux and Cheyenne as a location for the vision-quest.

Here Brooke Medicine Eagle underwent the traditional preparation of fasting and cleansing. She was expecting to spend up to four days and nights alone on a mountain top, without food and water, praying for her initiatory vision.

After preparing a sage-bed, smoking a pipe and offering prayers, the women departed and Brooke Medicine Eagle was left alone. She recalls that in the evening, as she lay there peacefully, she suddenly became aware of the presence of another woman who had long black braided hair and was dressed in buckskin. She seemed to be imparting some sort of energy into her navel – the communication between them was not in words.

As clouds moved across the sky, allowing the moonlight to filter through, Brooke Medicine Eagle became aware of 'a flurry of rainbows' caused by hundreds of beads on the woman's dress. Now she could also hear drumming, and it seemed then that two circles of dancing women – 'spirits of the land' – surrounded her, and that these circles were interweaving with each other. One circle included seven old grandmothers, 'women who are significant to me, powerful old women'.[19]

Then the circles disappeared and once again she was alone with the Rainbow Woman. The woman now told her that the land was in trouble – that it needed a new sense of balance, and specifically more feminine, nurturing energy and less male aggression. She also said that all dwellers on the North American continent were 'children of the rainbow' – mixed-bloods – but that there could be a balancing between the old cultures and the new.

After they had spoken with each other in this way it was time for the Rainbow Woman to leave, and it now became abundantly clear that this being was a spirit teacher, not a tangible physical form:

> Her feet stayed where they were, but she shot out across the sky in a rainbow arc that covered the heavens, her head at the top of that arc. And then the lights that formed that rainbow began to die out, almost like fireworks in the sky, died out from her feet and died out and died out. And she was gone.[20]

For Brooke Medicine Eagle the impact of the visitation was both personal and profound, for the communication touched on the crucial distinction between Native American and Western ways, and also indicated how she could be of service.

> The Indian people are the people of the heart. When the white man came to this land, what he was to bring was the intellect, that analytic, intellectual way of being. And the Indian people were to develop the heart, the feelings. And those two were to come together to build a new age, in balance, not one or the other . . .

[The Rainbow Woman] felt that I would be a carrier of the message between the two cultures, across the rainbow bridge, from the old culture to the new, from the Indian culture to the dominant culture, and back again. And in a sense, all of us in this generation can be that. We can help bridge that gap, build that bridge into the new age of balance.[21]

This, then, is Brooke Medicine Eagle's particular path in shamanism. It is a path she treads with a special conviction, sure in the knowledge that the earth will benefit from more feminine energy, more caring. 'We need to allow, to be receptive, to surrender, to serve,' she says. 'The whole society, men and women, need that balance to bring ourselves into balance.'

SUN BEAR

A medicine-man of Chippewa descent, Sun Bear is by no means a typical shaman. He is comparatively New Age in his orientation, heads a communal organisation consisting mainly of non-Native Americans, has worked in Hollywood, has a thriving practice in workshops and vision-quests, and has written several books. And yet he is a man whose message has touched many hearts. As a medicine-man he feels, like Brooke Medicine Eagle, that his path is to reach out to other cultures and to share with them his vision for harmony on earth.

Sun Bear, or Gheezis Mokwa, was born in 1929 on the White Earth Reservation in northern Minnesota. As a young child he had a vision of a large black bear sheathed in a vivid array of rainbow colours. The bear looked steadfastly at him, stood on its hind legs and gently touched him on his head. In this way he got his name. He also learned native medicine ways from his uncles and his brothers but then left his reservation at the age of 15. He says he didn't actually practise the medicine path until he was 25 years old. Prior to that he had quite a different career. Sun Bear worked in the Midwest and Southwest pursuing an assortment of occupations, including farming fields and working variously in a cemetery, bakery and real estate office. However, all this time he was still studying Native American healing traditions.

Later he worked for ten years in Hollywood on such television programmes as *Brave Eagle*, *Broken Arrow* and *Bonanza* and had acting parts in several films. In 1961 he also began publishing a magazine called *Many Smokes* which was intended as a forum for Native American writers and as a means of assisting the ecological cause of Earth awareness. The magazine changed its name to *Wildfire* in 1983 and now publishes a broad range of articles encompassing holistic health, vision-quests, wilderness studies, herbalism and New Age philosophy.

After working for the Intertribal Council of Nevada as an economic development specialist, Sun Bear assisted in a Native Studies programme sponsored by the University of California at Davis, north of San Francisco. It was here, in 1970, that he founded the Bear Tribe. Most of the members were his former students from the Davis campus. Sun Bear maintains that he selected the name because 'The Bear is one of the few animals that heals its own wounds' and he had in mind an organisation whose members 'could all join together to help with the healing of the Earth'.[22]

For a time the Bear Tribe resided near Placerville, California, but it is now located on a 100-acre farm amidst luxuriant evergreens close to Vision Mountain, 35 miles from Spokane in Washington. Sun Bear often isn't there – he now has an international workshop schedule which has taken him as far afield as Germany, Holland, England, India and Australia – but he has several able assistants who help to maintain the momentum. These include his wife, Wabun, formerly Marlise Ann James – a Master's graduate from the Columbia School of Journalism – and Shawnodese, who worked as a health inspector in Idaho prior to organising the Bear Tribe's Medicine Wheel gatherings. The community in Spokane is largely self-sufficient, has an extensive range of livestock, grows much of its own food and encourages self-reliance. Its workshop programme is extensive – an estimated 10,000 people attend Bear Tribe programmes each year – and the organisation has a 30,000 mailing list. There is no doubting that the Bear Tribe is an impressive operation.

Likewise, it would be easy to dismiss Sun Bear as an opportunist who has blended American Indian culture and modern American capitalism. However, several factors tell against this. Firstly, he doesn't draw a salary, and also, like other members of the Tribe, he assists in the menial tasks that have to be done on the farm. The Bear Tribe also offers work opportunities to the unemployed. Nevertheless, Sun Bear does not believe in turning his back on modern advances. 'I don't cling to any particular old way or ritual,' he told journalist Robert Neubert, 'nor do I believe that technology is necessarily bad: it's the greed and misdirection of its users that does harm. So the Bear Tribe isn't going back to the Stone Age. It's moving forward into the New Age.'[23]

But what of Sun Bear's personal vision? To what extent does he align himself with the traditional medicine path?

Sun Bear has summed up his philosophy as being one which teaches others to 'walk in balance on the Earth Mother'. In his book *The Medicine Wheel* he says: 'We all share the same Earth Mother, regardless of race or country of origin, so let us learn the ways of love, peace and harmony and see the good paths in life.'[24]

For Sun Bear, it is no longer appropriate to restrict the Native American teachings only to his own people. His view is truly global and he feels very strongly that his message is one of helping restore a sense of balance, of increased ecological awareness:

> If you teach people to find a better balance within themselves, how to be stronger, centre their life, and go forward with a good balance upon the Earth Mother, then that is a healing. You take away all the little pains when you teach people to become self-reliant. . . . When people have centred themselves, they know that they can draw power from the universe.[25]

Despite his apparently New Age emphasis, Sun Bear draws strongly on authentic Native American traditions. He shows group participants how to undertake a vision-quest – which includes fasting, prayers and ritual cleansing in a sweat-lodge: 'a symbolic act of entering the womb of the Mother to be reborn'. Four days and nights are then spent on the sacred mountain in isolation – some try to stay awake during this time but others allow themselves to fall asleep, hoping that mystical revelations will appear in their dreams.

But underlying all this, as Sun Bear explains, is an attitude of openness. One has to be able to receive the spirit, to cast aside the old restrictive programming. Accordingly, one of the practices prior to journeying to the sacred mountain is to dig a hole, pour into it one's anger or frustration, and then cover the hole over again with dirt and a prayer. Then it is a matter of going to a location where Earth Mother feels strong, where the energy seems vibrant, and where spirits might appear. It is the presence of spirits, in dreams or in visions, that provides an authentic sense of personal direction. But largely this is up to oneself. As Sun Bear says: 'Each medicine-man has to follow his own medicine and the dreams and visions that give him power.'

Another way of attracting the spirits is to don an animal mask, for example that of a buffalo, bear or eagle. By doing this, one feels a strong surge of spiritual energy, a profound sense of transformation: 'You literally become that entity, that power. . . . The spirit comes into you completely, to the extent that you are no longer there, and you are able to communicate what that spirit is feeling. That is what the ceremonies are about at the deepest depth.'[26]

One can definitely tell when the spirits have arrived, says Sun Bear: 'Sometimes it is just little whisperings, and sometimes a different energy, a change in the air that you feel, it is very recognisable.' One then begins to communicate on a different level of awareness: 'You feel and experience things as an energy that comes through the spirit forces at the time.'[27]

Sun Bear believes that, as a medicine-man, he is a protector of the Earth Mother, and an embodiment of the spirits of the earth. The resurgence of interest in shamanism is a reflection of the fact that humankind has increasingly fallen out of harmony with Nature. This is where Sun Bear feels he has a special role to play. His aim, when working with participants on vision-quests is 'to teach them how to make prayers and ceremonies for communication with the natural forces, so that they can start learning to restore their own power'.[28]

7 · Two
Controversies

For many years shamanism has been undergoing a resurgence of interest in the West and, as we have seen, is represented by an intriguing diversity of exotic personalities and approaches. However, there is no doubting that this revival owes much to the efforts of one man who has himself remained an enigma: the best-selling author, Carlos Castaneda. There has been extensive debate about the authenticity of his work – numerous books and articles have been written both to support and criticise his writings – and he has been mischievously compared with literary hoaxer Cyril Henry Hoskins, the Englishman better known through his alter ego, Lobsang Rampa. Be that as it may, through the impact of his internationally published books, the influence of Carlos Castaneda has been considerable. One can argue that, the academic efforts of scholar Mircea Eliade notwithstanding, Castaneda was the first person to make the shamanic perspective accessible to Westerners. It therefore seems appropriate here to include an overview of the man and the controversy he has aroused.

The Carlos Castaneda Debate

Between 1959 and 1973 Carlos Castaneda, an elusive South American given to wearing conservative three-piece suits, undertook a series of degree courses in anthropology at the University of California, Los Angeles. Although his real name was Carlos Arana, or Carlos Aranha, and he came either from Lima, Sao Paulo or Buenos Aires, he had adopted the name Carlos Castaneda when he acquired United States citizenship in 1959. The following year, having commenced his studies, he apparently travelled to the American Southwest to explore the Indian use of medicinal plants. As the story goes, a friend introduced him to an old Yaqui Indian who was said to be an expert on the hallucinogen peyote.

The Indian, don Juan Matus, said he was a *brujo*, a term which connotes a sorcerer, or one who cures by means of magical techniques. Born in Sonora, Mexico, in 1891, he spoke Spanish 'remarkably well' but appeared at the first meeting to be unimpressed with Castaneda's self-confidence. He indicated, however, that Castaneda should come to see him subsequently, and an increasingly warm relationship developed as the young academic entered into an 'apprenticeship' in sorcery.

Carlos Castaneda found many of don Juan's ideas and techniques strange and irrational. The world of the sorcerer contained mysterious, inexplicable forces that he was obliged not to question, but had to accept as a fact of life. The apprentice sorcerer would begin to 'see' whereas previously he had merely 'looked'. Eventually he would become a 'man of knowledge'.

According to Castaneda's exposition of don Juan's ideas, the world that we believe to be 'out there' is only one of a number of worlds. It is in reality a description of the relationship between objects that we have learnt to recognise as significant from birth, and which has been reinforced by language and the communication of mutually acceptable concepts. This world is not the same as the world of the sorcerer, for whereas ours tends to be based on the confidence of perception, the brujo's involves many intangibles. His universe is a vast and continuing mystery which cannot be contained within rational categories and frameworks.

In order to transform one's perception from ordinary to magical reality, an 'unlearning' process has to occur. The apprentice must learn how to 'not do' what he has previously 'done'. He must learn how to transcend his previous frameworks and conceptual categories and for a moment freeze himself between the two universes, the 'real' and the 'magically real'. To use don Juan's expression, he must 'stop the world'. From this point he may begin to *see*, to acquire a knowledge and mastery of the variable and mysterious forces operating in the environment which most people close off from their everyday perception.

'Seeing', said don Juan, was a means of perception which could be brought about often, although not necessarily, by hallucinogenic drugs – among them *mescalito* (peyote), *yerba del diablo* (Jimson Weed, or datura) and *humito* (psilocybe mushrooms). Through these, the brujo could acquire a magical ally, who could in turn grant further power and the ability to enter more readily into 'states of non-ordinary reality'. The brujo would become able to see the 'fibres of light' and energy patterns emanating from people and other living organisms; to encounter the forces within the wind and sacred water-hole, and isolate as visionary experiences – as if on film – the incidents of one's earlier life and their influence on the development of the personality. Such knowledge would enable the brujo to tighten his defences as a warrior. He would know himself, and have complete command over his physical vehicle. He would be able to project his consciousness from his body into images of birds and animals, thereby transforming into a myriad of magical forms and shapes while travelling in the spirit-vision.

Four of Carlos Castaneda's early books told of his magical apprenticeship to the sorcerer: *The Teachings of Don Juan*, *A Separate Reality*, *Journey to Ixtlan* and *Tales of Power*. The first of these included details of visionary encounters with the peyote god Mescalito, astral transformations in the form of a crow, and sessions ingesting datura and smoking sacred mushrooms. There were also accounts of unusual desert skills such as catching lizards and threading their eyelids with a cholla thorn needle.

On the face of it *The Teachings of Don Juan* seemed like a serious work, and it had, after all, been published by the University of California Press. However, from the beginning there were doubters and cynics.

To start with, no one, not even Castaneda's academic overviewing committee at UCLA, got to meet don Juan or even see a photograph of him; don Juan didn't fit the model of a regular Yaqui or have any discernible Indian characteristics; the manuscript was allegedly translated from Spanish fieldnotes since don Juan spoke in this tongue, but no fieldnotes were ever forthcoming; no Yaqui had ever been known to use datura, and sacramental mushroom rites were unknown in the region where Castaneda was said to have done his fieldwork.

Very early on, some anthropologists were highly critical. Peyote specialist Weston La Barre described Castaneda's second book, *A Separate Reality* as 'pseudo-profound, deeply vulgar pseudo-ethnography' and when Gordon Wasson wrote to Castaneda requesting detailed background data, he received only half-baked replies.

In more recent times another writer, Richard De Mille, has made something of an industry in debunking Carlos Castaneda in rigorous detail. De Mille is a former clinical psychologist who taught at the University of California, Santa Barbara, and since 1970 has worked as a writer and editor. His initial entry into Castaneda's 'ring of power' was with a work titled *Castaneda's Journey*, published in 1975, that quietly, and with an undoubted element of humour, tore strips off the 'non-ordinary' paradigm of truth Castaneda was proposing.

It raised serious linguistic questions about whether such phrases as 'I ran like the son of a bitch' and 'Don't lose your marbles' had any shaman-Spanish equivalent, pointed out numerous apparent inconsistencies in Castaneda's diary entries – some of them crucial to the acquisition of new magical skills learnt from the sorcerer – and also provided clues that Castaneda may have borrowed from other sources.

De Mille followed up on some of Gordon Wasson's linguistic objections to don Juan and sent a questionnaire to twenty-four linguistic experts detailing twenty-eight suspect phrases like those mentioned above. In compiling the replies, De Mille found that 59 per cent of the items were thought to have an English-language origin and most certainly had not been translated from Spanish.

De Mille's attack on the validity of the Castaneda books was not purely linguistic, however. One of his main points of contention was that Castaneda, in writing his account in the form of a diary, got all his chronologies mixed up.

As we have noted earlier, one of don Juan's key magical techniques was *seeing*. *Seeing*, wrote Castaneda, involved understanding that potentially 'anything can happen in the world and the magician is one who, like a warrior, can take his stand against the totally inexplicable.'

In *A Separate Reality*, Carlos asked don Juan: 'What is it like to see . . .' but don Juan told him that it must remain a secret for the time being. The Diary entry was May 1968. Meanwhile, *Journey to Ixtlan* provided a flashback to 1962, whereby Castaneda magically located an invisible bush growing in isolation on the side of a hill. 'This spot', said don Juan, 'is yours. This morning you *saw*, and that was the omen. You found this spot by *seeing*.'

In De Mille's view such incongruities raised serious doubts about the authenticity of the accounts. He was particularly suspicious about the sewing of the lizards' eyelids, since at the time of the event, it was nearly dark. In *Castaneda's Journey* he writes:

You who have passed a steel needle and a polished thread in bright light through a piece of inert but paper-thin leather about as wide as a newborn baby's little fingernail without ripping it will, I am sure, appreciate Carlos' skill in passing a perforated cholla thorn trailing an agave fibre in the darkening twilight through the tiny blinking membranes that shield a living lizard's eyes, without tearing them, never having tried it before, and never having seen anyone else do it before.

De Mille wondered where Castaneda could have dug up such an impossible skill, meanwhile presenting it as an accomplished fact. His conclusion about that particular incident was that it was a rewrite of an entry in *The Handbook of South American Indians*, which describes the sewing of a toad's eyes and mouth by a skilled Peruvian sorcerer.

Two things apparently really rankled with De Mille. The first was that Castaneda was awarded a PhD from UCLA for the third book, *Journey to Ixtlan*. The second was that when De Mille questioned the wisdom of the University of California Press in publishing Castaneda and put his own *Castaneda's Journey* forward to explain why, he was told that his book did not present an 'effective critique' because of its 'self-indulgent style and parodistic hypotheses'.

Nevertheless, the book's rejection may have been at least partially motivated by internal politics at UCLA. For example, De Mille raised some interesting insights into the power structures of the academic staff at UCLA. While staff members who passed Castaneda's dissertation initially were later unwilling to be drawn into debate on its merits, it became increasingly clear that the PhD was pushed through by Professor Harold Garfinkel, a scholar personally devoted to the view that reality is socially constructed. Garfinkel asked Castaneda to rewrite his thesis three times, and one of Garfinkel's colleagues, Arnold Mandell, said he felt that Castaneda rose to the occasion by deliberately submitting an imaginary ethnography. This suggested Castaneda was the true magician, rather than don Juan . . .

In a later book, *The Don Juan Papers*, published in 1980, Richard De Mille continues the debate about Castaneda's academic credibility and showed that he was perhaps becoming rather obsessive in his pursuits. After comparing Castaneda with the Piltdown Hoax he even went to the trouble of writing to the publishers of *Contemporary Authors* to alter the 'misleading' data on Castaneda and correct, among other things, his birthdate – which he had established as 1925.

However, one of the most interesting features of De Mille's later book was a lengthy conversation with Barbara Myerhoff, who knew

Castaneda personally as a student and was similarly engaged in the study of shamanism. However, whereas Castaneda was claiming to be studying Yaqui sorcery, Myerhoff was specialising in the Huichol Indians and in particular in a spectacular shaman named Ramon Medina, whom Castaneda later met. It may be that Castaneda borrowed an incident in *A Separate Reality* – where don Juan's friend, don Genaro, leaps across a precipitous waterfall clinging to it by magical tentacles of power – from an actual Huichol occurrence.

Barbara Myerhoff and another noted anthropologist, Peter Furst, actually watched Ramon Medina leaping like a bird across a waterfall, which cascaded three hundred metres below, over slippery rocks. Medina was exhibiting the balance of the shaman in 'crossing the narrow bridge to the other world'. Myerhoff told De Mille how pleased she felt, in terms of validation, when Castaneda related to her how the sorcerer don Genaro could also do similar things. It now seems, she feels, that Castaneda had been like a mirror and his own accounts reflected borrowed data from all sorts of sources – including her own. The rapid mystical running known as 'the gait of power', for example, was likely to have come from accounts of Tibetan mysticism and there were definite parallels between don Juan's abilities and statements in other anthropological, psychedelic and occult sources.

However, while Castaneda was being relentlessly pursued by Richard De Mille, there were others who were willing to come to his aid. One was the distinguished authority on shamanism, Michael Harner – whose psychedelic initiation in the Amazon is described earlier in this book. Harner stated, quite correctly, that shamanic techniques of attaining ecstasy or passing through the cracks between the worlds were remarkably similar in *all* shamanic cultures. In other words, although Castaneda may have been borrowing, he wasn't inventing. The Castaneda books were, and are, essentially accurate accounts of how a shaman might be expected to act. Further still, Castaneda was to be thanked for bringing the awesome realities of the shaman's universe to the notice of the general public.

Michael Harner still holds to this view, and in *The Don Juan Papers* is quoted as describing Castaneda's work as '110 per cent valid since it conveys a deep truth, though his specific details [could] often be justifiably questioned'. Harner personally offered assistance in helping Castaneda place his manuscript in the 1960s, after a notable New York publisher declined it.

Harner is convinced that Castaneda's initial motive was certainly not to make a financial killing from a perpetrated hoax but that the later books probably became embellished as the popularity of the don Juan saga grew. Barbara Myerhoff has also confirmed that Carlos himself often acted like a shaman – performing a healing cure for colic on her young son and also wrestling with alien agencies in his basement flat, in what seemed almost like an internal metaphysical encounter with the forces of good and evil.

So what emerges from the Carlos Castaneda debate is that Carlos himself is probably the actual visionary and many of the shamanic perspectives have been implanted in the personage of the real, partially real, or unreal being known as don Juan. In this sense it hardly matters to the person interested in states of consciousness and perception whether don Juan is real or not since the fiction, if it is that, is authentic enough. It is nevertheless interesting that later Castaneda works, like his 1984 publication *The Fire From Within*, have been presented in some editions as 'novels'.

ENTER LYNN ANDREWS

It was perhaps inevitable that a feminine counterpart of Carlos Castaneda would appear, and in due course she did – in the form of Lynn V. Andrews. Like Castaneda, she too had elusive shaman-teachers, only hers were, predictably, women. Where Castaneda had don Juan and don Genaro, Andrews had Ruby Plenty Chiefs and Agnes Whistling Elk. Whereas Castaneda was stalked by a fierce female antagonist – La Catalina – Andrews had a formidable male adversary called Red Dog. And, like Carlos Castaneda, she too claimed that her experiences were completely genuine!

Unlike Castaneda, Lynn Andrews' personal history has been more forthcoming. Now in her late forties, she was raised on a ranch near Spokane and moved to Los Angeles with her family when she was 14. She studied psychology and philosophy at college, worked for a time as a stockbroker and in film-making, and then became an art-dealer in Beverly Hills, her life revolving around the moneyed glamour-set of Bel Air. It was while visiting Guatemala for an art client that her life changed.

She had flown to Guatemala City to locate a fertility sash for an art-collector. During her visit she also travelled to the Mayan ruins of Tikal-Peten, but while wandering in awe among the hieroglyphics of the Grand Jaguar Temple, she became lost. Fortunately a tall Indian man appeared, and she asked him for directions back to town. After the man had pointed the way she offered him a twenty-dollar note in gratitude. He then looked at her intently, as she recounts in *Medicine Woman*:

'This money that you have given me binds you,' he said. 'I will send you two helpers within forty-four days. The first helper will be female. You will not recognise her as your ally. This ally you must conquer. I will also send you a male helper, who will mark your trail.' He ripped the twenty dollar bill in half and gave half back to me, saying 'Keep this.'[1]

Andrews, somewhat perplexed, returned to Guatemala City – where she then located a sash from a trader – and flew back to Los Angeles.

Two months later, while visiting an exhibition devoted primarily to Stieglitz photographs, she was attracted to a McKinnley photograph of a very beautiful Indian basket – 'it had an intricate pattern resembling a dolphin with a snake, or with lightning'. That night she had the first of several mysterious dreams – in this one she was offered a 'marriage basket' by an Indian woman 'with eyes like polished mirrors'.

Next day, inspired by her dream, Andrews spoke with the art gallery, intent on purchasing the photograph she had seen earlier. She was amazed to be told that no such photograph existed. Thus continued the strange string of events which had begun to dominate her life.

Soon afterwards, Lynn Andrews attended a party in Bel Air where she met the noted shaman-writer Hyemeyohsts Storm, author of *Seven Arrows*. She was able to ask him about the marriage basket, and Storm replied that he had seen only one in his life and was no longer sure who owned it. If Andrews wanted to find out, she would have to contact an old *heyoka*, or medicine-woman, called Agnes Whistling Elk on the Cree Reservation in Manitoba, Canada. If Agnes proved hard to find – she was often moving around – another woman called Ruby Plenty Chiefs, who also lived on the reservation, would know where to locate her.

As Andrews relates in *Medicine Woman*, she flew to Winnipeg, rented a car, and drove to the reservation north of Crowley, where she met Ruby Plenty Chiefs and went through a 'sort of initiation' with her. Ruby then put her into contact with Agnes Whistling Elk. Andrews says:

When I finally met her and saw that she was the woman in my dreams, I said, 'Agnes, what am I doing, why is this happening? I only wanted to buy the basket.' Agnes laughed and said, 'This basket can only be earned. It cannot be bought or sold. It is a very sacred object.' And she told me that it represented the symbol of the balance of the male and female within us all and with the healing of Mother Earth.[2]

88

As she later discovered, the actual marriage basket was in the possession of a sorcerer called Red Dog, who had no right to it. Andrews' challenge was now to help wrest the basket from his control, and the quest soon took on a deeper dimension. Her ensuing shamanic apprenticeship with Ruby Plenty Chiefs and Agnes Whistling Elk would have a profoundly transforming impact on her life, developing within her an intense magical resolve grounded in feminine spirituality.

However, if Andrews' shifting career-pattern seemed almost unbelievable, it was her claimed acceptance into an exclusive secret society of shaman women – the Sisterhood of the Shields – and her descriptions of native initiatory practices which have caused much of the controversy that now surrounds her writings.

In *Medicine Woman* Andrews says she was instructed to gut a deer and eat its still-warm heart, and on another occasion to strip naked before a group of native elders in a teepee. Such practices are totally unknown among the Manitoba Indians and have angered many members of the Cree community who have read her book. They also say that the names Agnes Whistling Elk and Ruby Plenty Chiefs are totally lacking in authenticity.

Following on from this, the editors of the Mohawk Indian newspaper, *Akwesasne Notes*, published in Ontario, listed Lynn Andrews in 1987 as one of several 'plastic medicine men and women' who are engaged on speaking tours and who charge gullible white people for their performances.

While Lynn Andrews no longer undertakes lecture tours and has switched instead to one-to-one shamanic counselling, the controversy surrounding her publications still continues. Andrews followed the best-selling *Medicine Woman* – first released in 1981 – with a number of highly successful sequels, including *Flight of the Seventh Moon, Jaguar Woman, Star Woman* and, more recently *Crystal Woman* – an account of her shamanic involvement with the Australian Aborigines. Here too, she appeared to strike difficulties – her account once again stretching credibility.

Andrews says in *Crystal Woman* that Agnes Whistling Elk came with her to Australia and that they travelled with an Aboriginal woman called Ginevee to a special ceremonial centre, 150 miles from Ayers Rock in the Northern Territory:

> Our destination was a little-known village where many Aboriginal women of high degree or healers were gathered to share their ancient knowledge with apprentices and each other. Their meeting was held in

secret, Agnes told me, because there were many warrior societies who were against such a gathering of female power.[3]

Andrews also describes an initiation where a large gathering of Aboriginal women came together and her naked body was smeared with bandicoot grease. However, this description has baffled local residents and authorities on Aboriginal culture. Mr Yami Lester, Chairman of the Pitjantjatjara Council has confirmed that there was no record of Lynn Andrews' visit to the Pitjantjatjara lands in Central Australia and that no one had any memory of her visit. Mr Lester also noted that he had never heard of an Aboriginal name like Ginevee, that bandicoots hadn't been seen in these lands for thirty years, and that members of the Women's Council found her ceremony 'laughable'. Furthermore, a word for Aborigines used in her book, Koori, referred not to Central Australian Aborigines but to the Aborigines of Victoria and New South Wales. Perhaps most damning of all, though, were the Immigration Department records: Lynn Andrews had visited Australia for only two weeks, between 24 June and 9 July 1986 – hardly time for more than a cursory visit. It was apparent that Andrews had little first hand knowledge of the Aborigines, and it clearly showed in her book.[4]

So, like Castaneda, there appear to be major questions surrounding the writings of Lynn Andrews. But what are we to make of her own shamanic viewpoint? If the specific details of her initiations and magical exploits appear to raise more questions than they answer, are there nevertheless useful insights which flow from the woman herself?

As with Castaneda, Lynn Andrews' personal philosophy proves to be worth hearing, if somewhat coloured by the particular milieu she is catering to.

When one places Lynn Andrews in the context of the many books on women's spirituality which have appeared in recent times – including Merlin Stone's When God was a Woman, Barbara G. Walker's Encyclopedia of Women's Mysteries, Starhawk's The Spiral Dance and Dreaming the Dark and Z. Budapest's The Holy Book of Women's Mysteries, among many others – it becomes much more obvious where Lynn Andrews' true passion lies. Her task is essentially to promote shamanism as a form of 'women's mysteries', to accord to women the role of restoring a sacred perspective to the planet.

In an interview published in Magical Blend magazine in 1987, Lynn Andrews made her personal orientation abundantly clear:

the indigenous cultures of this world know about Mother Earth, and that is why I was drawn to it . . . Shamanism, having to do with the balance of the Mother Earth, is something that is probably the answer to the world problem today. And I think that the burden of responsibility lies on women of the west.[5]

After pointing out that the energy of the earth is inherently female, she went on to say:

Women are the hope of the world, because if they will take power in a true and honest way – a feminine way – then they can teach men how to live and bring balance back onto the earth.

Andrews also seems intent on claiming that shamanism is a type of universal language which can be readily understood by any member of the Sisterhood of the Shields. In *Magical Blend* she asked:

Why is it that I can go to a shaman in Tibet or a shaman in Lapland, where I don't speak their language, and yet we communicate perfectly because the spirit language is the same. The source of power is always the same – it is female.[6]

In a chapter in the recently published *Shape Shifters: Shaman Women in Contemporary Society*, Andrews also implies that the Sisterhood is a unified secret movement – a spiritual undercurrent with a common goal:

The Sisterhood of Shields is a secret society of women who work towards self-realisation. The society is based on the ancient traditions of women. Although originally the members were all Native Americans, because of the needs of the time, women of other races are now initiated into the Sisterhood. As we share our wisdom we help bring a balance to the planet . . .

The interesting thing to me is that in all native traditions, whether from Australia, Africa, Canada or the Yucatan, the language is the same.

We communicate without words because the basic life-force energy emanates from Mother Earth . . . we can still communicate across cultural existence. I think that's the important thing about the Sisterhood of Shields. It isn't just focused on one tradition. We really do cross-pollinate everything we have across the world.[7]

Such a message obviously has a great emotive power, despite the fact that it is anthropologically simplistic. It also conveys the impression that male energies necessarily play a lesser role in shamanism. While for most contemporary writers on shamanism gender issues are less important than the exploration of mythic consciousness in general, Andrews has unfortunately polarised her viewpoint in a specific direction. Her books reflect an apparently personal need to find a secret, feminine society promoting shamanism in every culture she visits (albeit briefly) and are thus more of a projection of her own desires than an authentic account of what really exists.

And yet Lynn Andrews' personal philosophy stems from an obviously deeply felt intuition that the world needs a rapid dose of enhanced planetary awareness, and that one can address this both individually and collectively:

> The reason that I teach shamanism is because psychology doesn't really teach you to be your own teacher. I think that we have to look deeply within ourselves to that still point, to begin to see our own reflections and study them.
>
> What I do is take people down to the essence. I look at all the layers of conditioning, like layers of an onion. I tear the layers down so that you can get down to what you're really afraid of. Otherwise with all the covering you don't have a chance to see the world as it really is. The vision is veiled. The process of enlightenment is tearing the veils away.[8]

And on a broader basis, as a type of urban shaman, she makes this point:

> We are no longer hunting for buffalo; we are trying to survive a nuclear age and we are trying to bring wisdom into a new way of consciousness. . . . We may not have the opportunity to have any traditions at all if we don't heal Mother Earth now.[9]

Here, I suspect, we are hearing the real Lynn Andrews. It may well be that she could have come to this position – a powerful summation of the relevance of shamanism in the world today – without the support of her more questionable writings.

These words, at least, ring true.

8 • SHAMANISM IN THE WEST

If Carlos Castaneda, and more recently Lynn Andrews, have done much to attract popular attention to shamanism – albeit arousing a certain amount of controversy in the process – then it is also appropriate to acknowledge a potentially much more significant contribution: the work of Professor Michael Harner.

Whereas Castaneda and Andrews occupy a somewhat tenuous position on the shamanic spectrum, Harner has impeccable credentials, both as an academic and as a practising shaman. Without doubt (since the recent death of Mircea Eliade) the world's leading authority on shamanism, Harner has been a visiting professor at Columbia, Yale and the University of California at Berkeley, as well as Associate Professor of the New School for Social Research in New York. But he has also experienced the world of the shaman firsthand. He has studied the shamans of the Wintun, Pomo, Coast Salish, Lakota Sioux and Jivaro, and it was with the Conibo Indians of the Peruvian Amazon that he experienced the initiatory vision described in Chapter 4. Harner, more than anyone else, has helped to lift the practice of shamanism away from the domains of specialist anthropology and located it firmly within the human potential movement. As such he has helped make the experience of the shamanic reality more accessible to Westerners. The method he presents is essentially a synthesis adapted for a Western audience, while still remaining true to the principles of mainstream shamanism, and does not utilise psychedelics.

Harner's workshops – presented mainly at meetings organised by the International Transpersonal Association, at Esalen Institute and at other 'growth' centres in the United States and Europe – feature the beating of a large flat drum which the person taking the role of shamanic voyager uses as a vehicle to travel into the 'mythic world'. The participant relaxes in darkness, or with the eyes closed, and visualises a majestic tree whose branches reach up towards the heavens and whose roots extend deep into the earth. As the drumming begins the technique is to imagine that you are entering a doorway at the foot of the tree and then feel as if you are passing into one of the large roots – which then becomes a tunnel through to light which is perceived at the other end. The shaman now journeys toward the light, feeling all the time that the drumbeat is providing a sense of propulsion, and passes through into the luminous haze beyond. At this stage the participant now 'calls' for a guide – an animal, spirit being or mythic creature – who can assist in the exploration of the shamanic realm of consciousness which is now accessible. The journeys lasts for around twenty minutes – although one often has the feeling that the journey is 'beyond time' – and ends when a special drumbeat signal calls the voyager home. It is then a matter of recalling and recording as many details of the shamanic journey as possible, and perhaps sharing them with a friend.

Harner believes that the monotonous drum rhythms produced during a shamanic session activates theta patterns in the brain (associated with creative thought) and also simulate the rhythmic beating of the heart. When I asked him in an interview in 1984 about the physiology of the drumbeat in shamanism he had this to say:

> There have been very few scientific studies so far on what happens to a shaman making the journey. We need much more of this kind of research. But in one research project that was done using electro-encephalographic equipment to measure brain-waves it was found that the shaman in just ten minutes of journeying achieved a state of consciousness, empirically, scientifically measured, that had only been duplicated once before and that was by Japanese Zen masters in deep meditation after six hours of work. So the effect of the

drumming, as well as the shamanic methods, is very, very considerable.[1]

Michael Harner has also taught Westerners how to apply the healing powers of shamanism – which go beyond the purely self-developmental aspects of the process. In these workshops the favoured technique is that of the 'spirit canoe'. Here, the participants – ideally there may be between twelve and fifteen – sit on the floor in a canoe-configuration and face the same direction: the person in need of healing – a person who in a true sense is dis-spirited – lies in the centre of the 'canoe'. At the same time one of the group members sits at the rear, ready to beat the drum. The drumming will enable the participants to focus their energies towards the healing purpose at hand.

The healer-shaman, meanwhile, uses a rattle to define the sacred space wherein the transformation will occur. Gourd rattles are used to announce the shamanising and to summon the 'healing spirits'.

The shaman now enters the spirit canoe and lies down beside the sick person. His task, once the drumming begins, is to journey into the magical world to find a power animal (or source of spiritual energy) for his dis-spirited client. Having signalled for the drumming to commence, the shaman focuses his consciousness, accompanied by the collective will-to-heal of the members riding in the spirit canoe, and prepares to journey to the 'other world'. As mentioned earlier, the shaman rides on the drumbeat and visualises a tunnel leading to the magical domain. Here he looks for an animal which, according to shamanic tradition, presents itself to view from four different directions.

Once the animal has appeared, the shaman's role is to clasp it to his chest, and, imaginally, to return with it to the everyday world. He now kneels beside the sick person, signifying to the client to sit upright, and 'breathes' the animal into the patient's head through cupped hands. Lowering the sick person down to the floor again, he then breathes the animal into the chest.

The Shaman whispers to the client, 'I have given you an antelope' or 'I have given you a hare', depending on which creature has presented itself, and the formerly dis-spirited person prepares to rise and 'dance' the newly received power-animal to the accompaniment, once again, of the drumbeat.

For the recipient of shamanic healing the shamanising can produce a dramatic emotional transformation at this time. When the dance is concluded the shaman steps out of the 'canoe', signals to the four quarters with his rattles, and the healing ceremony is completed.

Cinetel Productions

Michael Harner and a 'spirit canoe' healing workshop

A SHAMANIC WORKSHOP

Tonight the shamanic workshop is being held at 'Kiva' – a large open room in an old tenement building in Canal Street, lower Manhattan. Most of the participants have experienced the shamanic journey before and are familiar with 'riding' the drumbeat into a state of meditative trance. They are wearing casual, comfortable clothing and have brought cushions and blankets, as well as handkerchiefs to drape over their eyes.

The session begins as Harner shakes his gourd rattle to the four quarters, summoning the 'spirits' to participate in the shamanic working. He also encourages the group to chant the Jivaro shaman-song:

> I have spirits,
> Spirits have I . . .
> I have spirits,
> Spirits have I . . .
> I have spirits,
> Spirits have I . . .
> I, I, I

The participants, meanwhile, have formed themselves into the shape of a 'spirit-canoe' – and each person present will visualise themselves riding in it, sailing down to the 'lower world'.

A dis-spirited woman named Regina lies in the centre of the canoe, and it is for her that the shamanising will be done. After the initial procedures, Harner will join the canoe, lie beside her, and endeavour to journey on her behalf to the magical world. There he will obtain a healing spirit which can be transferred to her body, revitalising her and making her well again.

Harner completes his circle of the spirit-canoe, lays down his gourd rattle and rests beside Regina. A young man seated at the rear of the canoe now begins to drum. It is a regular and monotonous drumbeat, deliberately intended to simulate the gallop of a horse and the rhythm of the heart.

The shaman and his helpers in the spirit-canoe now visualise the vessel passing down into the earth through 'the crack between the worlds'. In shamanic belief, as we noted earlier in this book, man lives on Middle Earth and the two magical domains – the upper and lower universes – are accessible through the trance journey. Often, as experienced shamanic explorers report, the upper and lower worlds tend to merge into a single 'magical reality' which parallels the familiar world. It is here that the shaman must seek a power animal which is willing to offer a new spirit of vitality to Regina.

The sonorous drumming continues, intensifying its rhythm. Harner, meanwhile, has succeeded in locating a spirit in the lower world and clutches it symbolically to his chest. He now rises to his knees still clasping the 'creature' in his hands. The drumming stops as he motions to Regina to sit up. Cupping his hands together above her head, Harner now 'blows' the spirit into her body. He repeats the same action over her chest, whispering to her, 'I have given you a deer', and Regina knows that she must acknowledge this gift in the ceremonial context.

She is a Yoruba black woman, well versed in ritual dance, and she is familiar with the concept of propitiating the healing spirits. Gracefully, ever gracefully, she dances around inside the spirit-canoe, welcoming the presence of the magical creature who has restored health and vitality to her body. With lilting gestures and a lyrical expression of form, she dances her power animal, a dance which is totally unstructured and expresses her inner feelings as they well up within her. Then the work is done. Regina sits down to rest, and Michael Harner announces to the group that the shamanic session is complete. Later Regina tells us how it felt to receive this gift of healing: 'Well, Michael is a very strong shaman,' she says, 'and when he gave me my power animal I felt a surge of energy. The dancing is very spontaneous. . . . I was letting go with all the energy he had breathed in.'

Other members of the group have made their own spirit journeys also – to other regions of the magical terrain. Some of these experiences reveal the extraordinary range of mythological images which become available through the shamanic process. One woman, for example, had ventured to the upper world:

> I was flying. I went up into black sky – there were so many stars – and then I went into an area that was like a whirlwind. I could still see the stars, and I was turning a lot, and my power animals were with me. Then I came up through a layer of clouds and met my teacher – who was a woman I'd seen before. She was dressed in a long, long gown and I wanted to ask her how I could continue with my shamanic work, how to make it more a part of my daily life. Then she took me up through her vagina, actually took me into her, into her belly. I could feel her get pregnant with me and felt her belly stretching. I felt myself inside her. I also felt her put her hands on top of her belly and how large it was! She told me that I should stop breathing, that I should take nourishment from her, and I could actually feel myself stop breathing. I felt a lot of warmth in my belly, as if it were coming into me, and then she stretched further and actually broke apart. Her belly broke apart and I came out of her, and I took it to mean that I needed to use less will in my work, and that I needed to trust her more and let that enter into my daily life. That was the end of my journey – the drum stopped and I came back at that point.[2]

Michael Harner believes that mythic experiences of this sort are common during the shamanic journey and reveal a dimension of consciousness rarely accessed in daily life:

> Simply by using the technique of drumming, people from time immemorial have been able to pass into these realms that are normally reserved for those approaching death, or for saints. These are the realms of the upper and lower world where one can get information to puzzling questions. This is the Dreamtime of the Australian Aboriginal, the 'mythic time' of the shaman. In this area, a person can obtain knowledge that rarely comes to other people.[3]

This of course begs the question of whether the shaman's journey is just imagination? Is the mythic experience *really* real? Harner's reply is persuasive:

Imagination is a modern Western concept that is outside the realm of shamanism. 'Imagination' already prejudges what is happening. I don't think it is imagination as we ordinarily understand it. I think we are entering something which, surprisingly, is universal – regardless of culture. Certainly people are influenced by their own history, their cultural and individual history. But we are beginning to discover a map of the upper and lower world, regardless of culture. For the shaman, what one sees – that's *real*. What one reads out of a book is secondhand information. But just like the scientist, the shaman depends upon first-hand observation to decide what's real. If you can't trust what you see yourself, then what can you trust?[4]

Harner is now deeply committed to shamanic research, and his workshops at Esalen, in New York, and in Germany and Austria, have become increasingly popular. In the summer of 1984 he spoke on shamanism at the Academy of Sciences of the USSR in Moscow, attracting the largest audience for a foreign visitor in four years. But the work hasn't stopped there. He is now engaged also in training native tribal peoples in shamanic techniques which have disappeared from their own indigenous cultures. Several groups, including the Sami (formerly known as Lapps) and the Inuit (formerly known as Eskimo) have approached him to help them restore sacred knowledge lost as a result of missionary activity and European colonisation. Harner has been able to help them with what he calls 'core shamanism' – general methods consistent with those once used by their ancestors. In this way, he says, 'members of these tribal societies can elaborate and integrate the practices on their own terms in the context of their traditional cultures.'

CAN WE BE SHAMANS IN THE WEST?

It is one thing to experience the mythic states of consciousness accessed through shamanic drumming but quite another to claim that one is functioning as a shaman in society. What lessons, therefore, can we learn from shamanic practices, and to what extent can we apply the shamanic perspective in a modern urban setting?

Personally, I don't think it is either possible, or appropriate, to try to turn back the cultural clock. Shamanism is traditionally the religious expression of a nomadic era of hunter-gatherers but most of us, in the West, live in industrialised cities or towns, surrounded by numerous manifestations of a complex technology. Furthermore, unlike the wandering shaman prone to the vagaries of the weather and seasonal variations in food supply, we have a comparatively settled

*Shamanism in the West – a yearning for deep inner experience
(drawing by Martin Carey) The Woodstock Aquarian*

existence and, for the most part, buy our food in a supermarket or store. Shamanism originates in comparatively isolated, pre-literate societies and it would surely be partaking of a fantasy to endeavour to transpose the world of the shaman to our own contemporary setting in any literal way.

This point notwithstanding, it is always possible to find some Westerners on retreats, or engaged in personal growth workshops, who enjoy the theatre of dressing up – who believe that by donning Red Indian feather headdresses or by puffing a ceremonial pipe or burning sage, that they can take on a shamanic persona.

Clearly, for modern city-bound Westerners such practices are fraught with illusion – they are ultimately artificial, focusing on the external appearances of shamanism rather than the core inner, visionary experience. But having said that, I do believe that there is a basic world-view – an approach to our planetary existence – which can be transposed from traditional shamanism to the modern context.

It seems to me that the resurgence of interest in native mythologies, in altered states of consciousness, in the mysticism of the East – that all these things reflect a widespread yearning in the West for religious frameworks based on deep inner experience. Shamanism can certainly help us here. The symbolism of the Shaman-Tree, used in visualisation, is of universal appeal, and hardly implies an imposed belief system. The root-tunnel which leads towards the light is a motif of transition – one uses it to journey into a realm of consciousness which would otherwise be possibly inaccessible. Whether we call this level of awareness our 'subconscious mind' or our 'inner self', or use some other comparable term to describe it it is clear the the shamanic technique opens up the possibility for each of us to discover our *own* inner mythology, to explore our own transpersonal archetypes, to find our own Dreamtime. For here are our own inner gods – the voices of our soul – and by discovering them and by communicating with them we have access to a deep and often profound spiritual reality that bears its own sense of authenticity. We no longer require a formal religious framework or belief system based on some form of empty, inherited doctrine. Our religion, once again, has become based on what we can feel, what we can *know*.

Secondly, a universal aspect of shamanism – and a perception I believe we can all be enriched by, irrespective of our personal religious dispositions – is a feeling for the sheer 'alive-ness' of the universe. Gone is any distinction between animate or inanimate. The whole universe is ablaze with energy – a vibration, a flowing and ebbing, a pulsing. All forms are perceived as interconnected, with a universal life-force underlying all. This in turn becomes a truly holistic vision because energy is matter, matter is spirit – and our purpose in applying the shamanic orientation within our own lives then becomes one of finding for ourselves our individual role within the matrix, a way in which we can assist the Universal Flow.

Increasingly, the holistic health movement is urging us to discover our own inner truths, to heed our own inner voice – to take the responsibility for our actions. Certainly, like shamans, there are times when we will explore uncharted waters, encounter obstacles, and perhaps wander down blind alleys. But hopefully, at other times, we will also venture into sacred realms that are truly awesome and which extend well beyond familiar realms of consciousness. Some of us, no doubt, have experienced spaces like this already – through meditation, through prayer, or by exploring psychedelics – and the experience has often been profound and life-transforming.

Allied to this, and also reinforced by the shaman's approach, is the need we all have to find the god, and goddess, within ourselves – to seek for a healing balance of male and female energies within our being and, perhaps most importantly, to recognise the sanctity of Nature. Shamanism is, if nothing else, a religious perspective which venerates Nature and – in this modern era of Chernobyl, industrial pollution and the ever-threatening chloro-fluorocarbon hole within the ozone layer – shamanism urges us to attune our religious beliefs to working *with* Nature and not against her.

I believe, then, that one can act as a type of modern shaman by addressing these principles in our personal life. It is not so much a matter of theatre or ceremonial, but a shift in basic attitudes. Shamanism can teach us much, simply by leading us back to a core simplicity in our lives: the basic perception that we all share a common destiny on this planet, that we are all born of Mother Earth, and that ultimately we are accountable, both to each other and to future generations, if the precious balance between humankind and Nature is jeopardised.

To this extent, then, we can all be like shamans while also being true to ourselves. As Sun Bear has said: 'We all share the same Earth Mother, regardless of race or country of origin, so let us learn the ways of love, peace and harmony, and seek the good paths in life.'

It is a message that each of us can truly take to heart.

RESOURCES

The Center for Shamanic Studies,
Box 673, Belden Station,
Norwalk, Connecticut 06852,
USA

(Dr Michael Harner) ph: (203) 454 2827

The Ojai Foundation,
PO Box 1620,
Ojai, California 93023,
USA

(Dr Joan Halifax)

Mishakai Center for the Study of Shamanism,
PO Box 844,
Covelo, California 95428
USA

(Prem Das)

Shared Visions/Sound Choices,
2510 San Pablo Avenue,
Berkeley, California 94702,
USA
ph: (415) 845 2216

Transformative Arts Institute,
PO Box 387,
San Geronimo, California 94963,
USA
ph: (415) 488 4965

Dance of the Deer Foundation,
PO Box 699,
Soquel, California 95073,
USA
(Brant Secunda) ph: (408) 475 9560

The Bear Tribe,
PO Box 9167,
Spokane, Washington 99209,
USA
(Sun Bear) ph: (509) 326 6561

SHAMANIC EQUIPMENT

Taos Indian Drum Company,
PO Box 1916D,
Taos, New Mexico 87571,
USA
ph: (505) 758 3796

Pacific Western Traders,
305 Wool Street,
Folsom, California 95630,
USA
ph: (916) 985 3851

One World Products,
Box L,
Taos, New Mexico 87571–0599,
USA
ph: (505) 758 4144

DRUMMING TAPES (TO ACCOMPANY SHAMANIC TRANCE JOURNEYS)
Drumming for the Shamanic Journey (Michael Harner)
Available from The Center for Shamanic Studies (see above)
Journey by Water Drum
Available from the Transformative Arts Institute, PO Box 6564,
  Albany, California 94706, USA
Shaman Journey (Nevill Drury)
Available from Listen Music, PO Box 996, Chatswood, NSW
  2067, Australia

PUBLICATIONS

Shaman's Drum magazine,
Box 2636,
Berkeley, California 94702,
USA
Magical Blend magazine,
PO Box 11303,
San Francisco, California 94101,
USA

Notes and
References

CHAPTER ONE: ANIMISM AND BEYOND

1   Abbé Henri Breuil, 'The Paleolithic Age', in René Huyghe (ed.) *Larousse Encyclopedia of Prehistoric and Ancient Art*, 1962, p. 30
2   Joan Halifax, *Shaman: the Wounded Healer*, 1982, p. 6
3   Ibid., p. 14
4   Ralph Linton, *Culture and Mental Disorders*, 1956, p. 124
5   Joan Halifax, op. cit., p. 14
6   Waldemar Bogoras, *The Chukchee*, 1909, p. 421
7   See H. S. Sullivan, *Conceptions of Modern Psychiatry*, Norton, New York, 1953, pp. 151–2
8   Mircea Eliade, *Shamanism*, 1972, p. 13
9   Mircea Eliade, *Birth and Rebirth*, 1964, p. 102
10 W. A. Lessa and E. Z. Vogt (eds.), *Reader in Comparative Religion*, 1972, p. 388
11 Ibid., p. 389

CHAPTER TWO: WHERE IS SHAMANISM FOUND?

1 Mircea Eliade, *Shamanism*, 1972, p.198
2 G. M. Vasilevich, 'Early Concepts about the Universe Among the Evenks', 1963, p. 58
3 Will Noffke, 'Living in a Sacred Way – an interview with Chequeesh, a Chumash Medicine Woman', 1985, pp. 13–17
4 See W. A. Lessa and E. Z. Vogt (eds.) *Reader in Comparative Religion*, 1972, Ch. 9.
5 Joan Halifax, *Shamanic Voices*, 1979, p. 183
6 In imitative magic the anticipated result in real life is mimicked, or imitated, in ritual – for example, the image of a real person may be subjected to hostile acts (pins, burning etc.). In contagious magic there is an implicit belief that objects that have been in contact with each other still have a link, and that one can be harmed magically – for example, by a magical rite performed over one's fingernails, hair clippings or possessions.
7 See A. P. Elkin's classic work, *Aboriginal Men of High Degree*, 1977, p. 63
8 H. L. Roth, *The Natives of Sarawak and British North Borneo*, 1968, Vol. 1, p. 281
9 Sue Ingram, 'Structures of Shamanism in Indonesia and Malaysia', 1972, p. 127
10 Kenneth Cohen, 'Taoist Shamanism', *The Laughing Man*, Vol. 2, No. 4, p. 49
11 Larry G. Peters, 'The Tamang Shamanism of Nepal', 1987, p. 171
12 For an account of Deguchi Onisaburo's trance experiences see Carmen Blacker, *The Catalpa Bow*, 1975.

CHAPTER THREE: SHAMANIC COSMOLOGIES

1 Mircea Eliade, *Shamanism*, 1972, p. 261
2 Ibid., p. 272
3 Ibid., p. 273
4 G. M. Vasilevich, 'Early Concepts about the Universe Among the Evenks', 1963
5 Asen Balikci, 'Shamanistic Behaviour Among the Netsilik Eskimos', 1967, p. 200
6 Joan Halifax, *Shamanic Voices*, 1979, p. 121
7 Ibid., p. 122

CHAPTER FOUR: RITUALS AND THE INNER WORLD

1   Weston La Barre, *The Ghost Dance*, 1972, p. 421
2   Ibid., p. 320
3   Michael Harner, *The Way of the Shaman*, 1980, p. 62
4   Mircea Eliade, *Shamanism*, 1972, p. 132
5   Carmen Blacker, *The Catalpa Bow*, 1975, p. 25
6   Joan Halifax, *Shamanic Voices*, 1979, p. 176
7   Ibid., p. 177
8   Michael Harner, op. cit., p. 51
9   Mircea Eliade, op. cit., p. 172
10   Ibid., p. 52
11   Joan Halifax, op. cit., p. 30
12   Nevill Drury, *Music and Musicians*, 1980, p. 51
13   Joan Halifax, op. cit., p. 30
14   Ibid., p. 185
15   Michael Harner, op. cit., p. 3

CHAPTER FIVE: SACRED PLANTS

1   Peter T. Furst, *Hallucinogens and Culture*, p. 112
2   Quoted in R. E. Schultes and A. Hofmann, *Plants of the Gods*,
     1979, p. 134
3   Ibid., p. 135
4   Peter T. Furst, op. cit., pp. 113–14
5   Prem Das, 'Initiation by a Huichol Shaman', pp. 18–19
6   R. G. Wasson, *The Wondrous Mushroom*, 1980, p. xvi
7   Henry Munn, 'The Mushrooms of Language' in Michael Harner
     (ed.) *Hallucinogens and Shamanism*, 1973, p. 88
8   Ibid., p. 90
9   R. E. Schultes and A. Hofmann, op. cit., p. 159
10   Peter T. Furst, op. cit., p. 72
11   Michael Harner, op. cit., p. 169
12   Peter T. Furst, op. cit., p. 48
13   Michael Harner, op. cit., p. 44
14   Peter T. Furst (ed.) *Flesh of the Gods*, 1972, p. 64
15   Douglas Sharon, 'The San Pedro Cactus in Peruvian Folk Heal-
     ing', 1972, p. 122
16   Ibid., p. 127
17   Ibid., p. 124
18   Ibid., p. 131
19   Ibid., p. 130
20   R. G. Wasson, op. cit., pp. 15–16
21   Ibid., p. 21

CHAPTER SIX: THE SHAMANS SPEAK

1 John G. Neihardt, *Black Elk Speaks*, 1972, p. 16
2 Quoted in Stephen Larsen, *The Shaman's Doorway*, 1976, p. 104
3 Ibid., p. 105
4 Ibid.
5 Ibid., p. 106
6 John G.Neihardt, op. cit., p. 35
7 Ibid., p. 36
8 Ibid., p. 39
9 Stephen Larsen, op. cit., p. 115
10 Ibid., p. 116
11 Personal communication, November 1984
12 Mimi Albert, 'Out of Africa', January/February 1987
13 Personal communication, November 1984
14 Mimi Albert, op. cit.
15 Michele Jamal, *Shape Shifters*, 1987, p. 164
16 Ibid., p. 165
17 Ibid., p. 164
18 Ibid., p. 162
19 Joan Halifax, *Shamanic Voices*, 1979, p. 68
20 Ibid., pp. 89–90
21 Michele Jamal, op. cit., pp..89–90
22 Robert Neubert, 'Sun Bear – Walking in Balance on the Earth Mother', p. 10
23 Ibid., p. 9
24 Sun Bear and Wabun, *The Medicine Wheel*, 1980, p. xiii
25 Ron Boyer, 'The Vision Quest', p. 63
26 Ibid., p. 60
27 Ibid., p. 61
28 Ibid., p. 62

CHAPTER SEVEN: TWO CONTROVERSIES

1 Lynn Andrews, *Medicine Woman*, 1981, p. 9
2 Richard Daab, 'An Interview with Lynn Andrews', 1987, p. 35
3 Peter Benesh, 'White Woman Write with Forked Typewriter', *The Sydney Morning Herald*, 2 July 1988, p. 25
4 Ibid.
5 Richard Daab, op. cit., p. 36
6 Ibid., p. 36
7 Michele Jamal, op. cit., pp. 25–6

8 Ibid., p. 24
9 Richard Daab, op. cit., p. 38

CHAPTER EIGHT: SHAMANISM IN THE WEST

1 Nevill Drury, interview with Michael Harner in November 1984, published in 'The Shaman: Healer and Visionary', *Nature and Health*, Vol. 9, No. 2, p. 86
2 Communication during filming for the documentary *The Occult Experience*, New York, November 1984
3 Ibid.
4 Ibid.

SELECT

BIBLIOGRAPHY

Albert, M., 'Out of Africa', *Yoga Journal*, January/February, 1987

Andrews, L., *Medicine Woman*, Harper & Row, San Francisco, 1981
    Flight of the Seventh Moon, Harper & Row, San Francisco, 1984
    Jaguar Woman, Harper & Row, San Francisco, 1985
    Star Woman, Warner Books, New York, 1986
    Crystal Woman, Warner Books, New York, 1987

Balikci, A., 'Shamanistic Behaviour Among the Netsilik Eskimos', in J. Middleton (ed.) *Magic, Witchcraft and Curing*, Natural History Press, New York, 1967

Bharati, A. (ed.), *The Realm of the Extra-Human*, Mouton, The Hague, 1976

Blacker, C., *The Catalpa Bow*, Allen & Unwin, London, 1975

Bogoras, W., *The Chukchee*, Memoirs of the American Museum of Natural History, Vol. XL, New York and Leiden, p. 421

Boyer, R., 'The Vision Quest', *The Laughing Man*, Vol. 2, No. 4

Breuil, H., 'The Paleolithic Age' in René Huyghe (ed.) *Larousse Encyclopedia of Prehistoric and Ancient Art*, Hamlyn, London, 1962, p. 30

Budapest, Z., *The Holy Book of Women's Mysteries*, Parts One and Two, Susan B. Anthony Coven #1 Coven, Los Angeles, 1979–80

Castaneda, C., *The Teachings of Don Juan*, University of California Press, Berkeley, 1968
> *A Separate Reality*, Simon & Schuster, New York, 1971
> *Journey to Ixtlan*, Simon & Schuster, New York, 1972
> *Tales of Power*, Simon & Schuster, New York, 1974
> *A Second Ring of Power*, Simon & Schuster, New York, 1976
> *The Eagle's Gift*, Simon & Schuster, New York, 1981
> *The Fire from Within*, Simon & Schuster, New York 1984

Cohen, K., 'Taoist Shamanism', *The Laughing Man*, Vol. 2, No. 4 p. 49

Daab, R., 'An Interview with Lynn Andrews', *Magical Blend*, No. 16, 1987

Das, P., 'Initiation by a Huichol Shaman', *The Laughing Man*, Vol. 2 No. 4

De Mille, R., *Castaneda's Journey*, Capra Press, Santa Barbara, 1976
> *The Don Juan Papers*, Ross-Erikson, Santa Barbara, 1980

Doore, G. (ed.), *Shaman's Path*, Shambhala, Boston, 1988

Drury, N., *Don Juan, Mescalito and Modern Magic*, Routledge & Kegan Paul, London, 1978
> *Inner Visions*, Routledge & Kegan Paul, London, 1979
> *Music and Musicians*, Nelson, Melbourne, 1980
> *The Shaman and the Magician*, Routledge & Kegan Paul, London, 1982
> *Vision Quest*, Prism, Dorchester, 1984
> *The Gods of Rebirth*, Prism, Bridport, 1988
> 'The Shaman: Healer and Visionary', *Nature & Health*, Vol. 9, No. 2
> *The Occult Experience*, Hale, London, 1987, and Avery, New York, 1989

Durkheim, E., *The Elementary Forms of the Religious Life*, Allen & Unwin, London, 1915

Eliade, M., *Birth and Rebirth*, Harper, New York, 1964
> *Shamanism*, Princeton University Press, New Jersey, 1972

Elkin, A., *Aboriginal Men of High Degree*, University of Queensland Press, St Lucia, Brisbane, 1977

Estrada, A., *Maria Sabina: Her Life and Chants*, Ross-Erikson, Santa Barbara, 1981

Furst, P. T. (ed.), *Flesh of the Gods*, Allen & Unwin, London, 1972
> *Hallucinogens and Culture*, Chandler & Sharp, San Francisco, 1976

Grof, S., *Realms of the Human Unconscious*, Dutton, New York, 1976

Halifax, J., *Shamanic Voices*, Dutton, New York, 1979
> *Shaman; The Wounded Healer*, Crossroad, New York, 1982

Harner, M., *The Jivaro*, Hale, London, 1972

Hallucinogens and Shamanism, Oxford University Press New York, 1973

The Way of the Shaman, Harper & Row, San Francisco, 1980

Hori, I., *Folk Religion in Japan*, University of Chicago Press, Chicago and London, 1968

Ingram, S., 'Structures of Shamanism in Indonesia and Malaysia', University of Sydney anthropology thesis, 1972

Jamal, M., *Shape Shifters*, Arkana, New York and London, 1987

Kalweit, H., *Dreamtime and Inner Space*, Shambhala, Boston, 1988

La Barre, W., *The Ghost Dance*, Allen & Unwin, London, 1972

Larsen, S., *The Shaman's Doorway*, Harper & Row, New York, 1976

Lessa, W. A. and Vogt, E. Z., *Reader in Comparative Religion*, Harper & Row, New York, 1972

Lewis, I., *Ecstatic Religion*, Penguin, Harmondsworth, 1971

Linton, R., *Culture and Mental Disorders*, Charles C. Thomas, Springfield, Illinois, 1956

Michael, H. N. (ed.), *Studies in Siberian Shamanism*, University of Toronto Press, Toronto, 1963

Middleton, J. (ed.), *Magic, Witchcraft and Curing*, The Natural History Press, New York, 1967

Munn, H., 'The Mushrooms of Language', in M. Harner (ed.), *Hallucinogens and Shamanism*, Oxford University Press, New York, 1973

Neihardt, J. G., *Black Elk Speaks*, Pocket Books, New York, 1972

Neubert, R., 'Sun Bear – walking in balance on the Earth Mother', *New Realities*, May/June 1987

Noel, D. (ed.), *Seeing Castaneda*, Putnam, New York, 1976

Noffke, W., 'Living in a Sacred Way: an interview with Chequeesh, a Chumash Medicine Woman', *Shaman's Drum*, Fall 1985

Nicholson, S. (ed.), *Shamanism*, Quest Books, Illinois, 1987

Oootorreich, T., *Possession*, University Books, New York, 1966

Peters, L. G., 'The Tamang Shamanism of Nepal' in S. Nicholson (ed.), *Shamanism*, Quest Books, Illinois, 1987

Roth, H. L., *The Natives of Sarawak and British North Borneo* (2 vols.), University of Malaya, Singapore, 1968

Schultes, R. E. and Hofmann, A., *Plants of the Gods*, Hutchinson, London, 1979

Sharon, D., 'The San Pedro Cactus in Peruvian Folk Healing', in P. T. Furst, *Flesh of the Gods*, Allen & Unwin, London, 1972

(with Eduardo Calderón, Richard Cowan and F. Kaye Sharon) *Eduardo el Curandero*, North Atlantic Books, Richmond, California, 1982

Starhawk, *The Spiral Dance*, Harper & Row, San Francisco, 1979

Dreaming the Dark, Beacon Press, Boston, 1982

Stone, M., *When God Was A Woman*, Dial Press, New York, 1976

Sun Bear and Wabun, *The Medicine Wheel*, Prentice-Hall, Englewood Cliffs, 1980

Teish, L., *Jambalaya*, Harper & Row, San Francisco, 1985

Tylor, E., 'Animism', in W. A. Lessa and E. Z. Vogt (ed.), *Reader in Comparative Religion*, Harper & Row, New York, 1972

Vasilevich, G. M., 'Early Concepts About the Universe Among the Evenks', in Henry N. Michael (ed.), *Studies in Siberian Shamanism*, University of Toronto Press, Toronto, 1963

Walker, B. G., *Encyclopedia of Women's Mysteries*, Harper & Row, San Francisco, 1983

Wasson, R. G., *Soma: Divine Mushroom of Immortality*, Harcourt, Brace Jovanovich, New York, 1968

The Wondrous Mushroom, McGraw Hill, New York, 1980

INDEX